Instructor's Resource Manual and Test Bank

The Psychology of Language

Paul Whitney
Washington State University

HOUGHTON MIFFLIN COMPANY   BOSTON   NEW YORK

Sponsoring editor: David C. Lee
Associate editor: Jane Knetzger
Senior Manufacturing Coordinator: Sally Culler
Marketing Manager: Pamela J. Laskey

Copyright © 1998 by Houghton Mifflin Company. All rights reserved.

Houghton Mifflin hereby grants you permission to reproduce the Houghton Mifflin material contained in this work in classroom quantities, solely for use with the accompanying Houghton Mifflin textbook. All reproductions must include the Houghton Mifflin copyright notice, and no fee may be collected to cover the costs of duplication. If you wish to make any other use of this material, including reproducing or transmitting the material or portions thereof in any form or by electronic or other mechanical means including any form of storage or retrieval system, you must obtain prior written permission from Houghton Mifflin Company, unless such use is expressly permitted by federal copyright law. If you wish to reproduce material acknowledging a rights holder other than Houghton Mifflin Company, you must obtain permission from the rights holder. Address inquiries to College Permissions, Houghton Mifflin Company, 222 Berkeley Street, Boston, MA 02116-3764.

Printed in the U.S.A.

ISBN: 0-395-75751-7

123456789-PA-02 01 00 99 98

Contents

Chapter 1 The Nature of Language — 1
Chapter 2 What Language Users Must Know — 11
Chapter 3 Language in Relation to Other Cognitive Processes — 21
Chapter 4 Theories of the Language-Thought Relationship — 31
Chapter 5 The Recognition of Spoken Words — 39
Chapter 6 Visual Word Recognition — 49
Chapter 7 Sentence Processing — 59
Chapter 8 Understanding and Remembering Discourse — 69
Chapter 9 Language Production and Conversation — 79
Chapter 10 Language Acquisition: Biological Foundations — 89
Chapter 11 Language Acquisition in Special Circumstances — 99
Chapter 12 Language and the Localization of Function — 107
References — 117

Preface

My purpose in preparing this resource manual and test bank is twofold. First, it gives me the opportunity to share with you how each chapter was designed to fulfill the objectives I had in mind in preparing *The Psychology of Language*. By giving you an insider's view of each chapter, I hope to make it easier for you to get as much out of using the text as possible. Second, in teaching both undergraduate and graduate students about psycholinguistics, and, especially, in writing *The Psychology of Language,* I have acquired some resources and techniques that might be useful to you. This manual gives me a chance to share these aids with you, and thereby make your job a little easier.

As I discuss the specific objectives and possible aids for each of the chapters, I'll relate the specific content back to the general objectives of the text. As you know, psycholinguistics is a technical and multidisciplinary field. As a consequence, it is easy for students to lose track of the major themes as they are confronted with many new terms and facts. By pointing the way back to the "big picture" as I discuss each chapter, I hope to help you keep the students aware of the way that key themes and issues run throughout the field.

It may take the students a bit of time to become accustomed to the idea that the chapters of the text are really organized around hypotheses not statements of fact. In some of the chapters, the bulk of the evidence supports the hypothesis in others it qualifies or refutes the hypothesis. My teaching experiences, as well as empirical research on learning from text, support the idea that using the information in the text to evaluate these hypotheses will promote learning of both thematic and detail information. Ultimately, of course, to know whether the course objectives are met, we have to measure students' achievement. To make this part of your job easier, I have included test bank items in this manual. The test items are intended to help you assess student mastery of both the factual and skill objectives that I had in mind in preparing the text.

I hope you find this manual helpful. I also hope that you will feel free to share your ideas and give me feedback on how various techniques have worked in your classroom. Although many of the ideas in this manual are based on my own experiences in teaching students about language, I have also included insights I've gained from the students themselves and from several anonymous reviewers of my book. If you have feedback or suggestions that you wish to share, you can reach me via e-mail at this address: pwhitney@mail.wsu.edu.

Chapter 1
The Nature of Language

Keeping an Eye on the Big Picture

The evaluation of the central organizing hypothesis for this chapter, the uniqueness of language, provides an opportunity to define what language is and what characteristics are shared by all languages. Of course, because many people have heard about Koko and the kitten or come into the course convinced that their pets have highly developed comprehension skills, it may take some effort during class discussions to get your students to view the data on the "animal language" question objectively. Even though I go to some pains in the chapter to separate the question of whether non-human animals possess language from the issue of the intrinsic value of these animals, many students need an active debate or discussion in order to use evidence rather than emotion to make a judgment.

Even though it is a difficult chore, taking on strongly held prior beliefs on the part of the students is an opportunity to begin two general lessons. One, students can start to see how data from unexpected sources can turn out to be quite relevant to a hypothesis. People can easily see the relevance of examining the behavior of specific animals to see if the animal possesses language. What many students do not see, at first, is why the issue of human evolution is critical if we are to know what conclusions we can, and cannot, draw from studying communication in various species. Two, the debate over the uniqueness of language is a good example of how we need to define our terms as precisely as possible when we evaluate a hypothesis. We cannot answer the question of whether language is unique to humans without defining what we mean by language. This seems obvious to the students when stated, but students seldom use definitions and criteria systematically when "in the heat of argument." That is a skill that must be practiced.

The Devilish Details

For each chapter, I'll try to help you anticipate which specific points will be the most difficult for the students to master and to point out some ways to help the students with techniques that augment the text's coverage. In the first chapter, there are three main sources of difficulty for the students: understanding the nature of evolution, appreciating the role of linguistic universals in the animal language debate, and understanding the concept of levels of analysis. I'll discuss each of these issues in turn.

Understanding Evolution

I find that my students vary a great deal in how much background they have on the subject of evolution. So, sometimes I have to provide more background than at other times. However, even

Copyright © Houghton Mifflin Company. All rights reserved.

bright students with good science training often have some important misconceptions about evolution that can interfere with understanding the discussion of evolution and language. Perhaps the most common and hard to combat of these misconceptions is the notion that evolution represents a path of progress toward perfection, with humans being the end point of "what evolution has been trying to accomplish." The "quiz" below can serve as a useful starting point for generating discussion on the nature of evolution, which gives you the opportunity to address common misconceptions.

Evolutionary Theory: A Quiz

For each item mark:
A. if the idea was part of pre-Darwinian biology
B. if the idea was part of Darwin's theory
C. if the idea is part of current evolutionary thinking
D. if none of the above are true

Mark each letter that applies.

_____ 1. Characteristics acquired during one's lifetime (e.g., increased muscle mass due to physical labor) can become inherited traits that lead to better adapted offspring.
_____ 2. Organisms tend to become more perfected over time.
_____ 3. The major driving force in evolution is natural selection.
_____ 4. The process of natural selection is fueled by *random* mutations.
_____ 5. Humans and apes share a common ancestor.
_____ 6. Organisms are adapted to their environments.
_____ 7. Natural selection moves organisms in the direction of greater complexity.
_____ 8. Natural selection makes organisms more adaptable to environmental changes.

Key:

1. A and B   2. A   3. B and, with some dissent, C   4. C   5. B and C   6. A,B,C
7. D. It can involve simplification and elimination of structures, as well.   8. D. It leads to greater adaptation to a particular environment, not necessarily environments in general.

You may also want to give the students some questions about human evolution and have them do research to find the answers. If you make this an Internet project, I suggest you steer the students to particular sites, because there is a lot of misinformation about human evolution on the Web. Two of the better sites are:
(1) The Origins of Humankind, http://www.dealsonline.com/origins/research/
(2) The *Scientific American* home page, http://sciam.com

Linguistic Universals

It is not so much that linguistic universals are hard to understand. Rather, they are sometimes hard to appreciate. I find that students come to a better appreciation for language universals when they are used as part of a comparative analysis. There are several ways to do this:

- You could make the "On Further Reflection" question 1 a formal assignment an discuss the results in class.
- The activity based on Premack's work (Activity 1.1) can be used as a discussion topic. Pose the question of how the symbol game would have to be modified or extended so that the use of these symbols would display each of the six universals discussed in the chapter.
- Assign as outside reading a report of results from one of the "ape language" projects. The papers from Sue Savage-Rumbaugh's lab, cited in the chapter, are good choices because she tends to include some reasonable samples of behavior. Have students evaluate the data in regard to whether the linguistic universals are in evidence.
- The segment on language from the PBS series, The Mind (produced by WNET, New York, 1988) has very compelling interviews with Jane Goodall and with David Premack. Their ideas on the cognitive and communication capacities of nonhuman primates could be analyzed in terms of the linguistic universals that are present and absent in these other species.

For each of these possible exercises, it is important to remind students that language is a complex ability with many dimensions. Thus, the question of whether a particular animal displays language or not is overly simplistic.

Levels of Analysis

The distinctions among Marr's levels are rather abstract, and many students struggle with the whole notion of levels. Nevertheless, to appreciate the difference between linguistics and psycholinguistics, and to appreciate what most of the studies in psycholinguistics are trying to accomplish, it is important for students to have some grasp of the differences among the levels. I find it useful to take something like the cash register problem (Activity 1.2) and work through what kinds of questions you could ask if you wanted to understand some system for processing information. The most difficult concept here seems to be the idea that you can have a functional model that is distinct from a consideration of the physical system. To clarify the idea of the representational level, you can take the exercise to the next step. Have students perform a simple language task, such as recognizing a word, and have them work through what questions could be asked at each level. You can then follow up on these questions as word recognition is discussed in later chapters.

Multiple Choice Test Items

1. The hypothesis that only humans use language suggests that

    a) only humans can use symbols to communicate.
    b) communication can only take place among members of the same species.
    c)* forms of animal communication are fundamentally different from human language.
    d) all of the above.

2. Vervet monkeys have distinctive calls that signify different predators (e.g., a leopard, rather than an eagle). This observation

    a)* suggests that animal communication may convey meaningful information.
    b) illustrates how human language evolved from the calls of earlier primates.
    c) is an example of an animal communication system that shows displacement.
    d) none of the above

3. According to current evolutionary theory, modern humans

    a) evolved from apes approximately 40,000 years ago.
    b) evolved from apes approximately 4 million years ago.
    c) evolved from apes approximately 150,000 years ago.
    d)* and apes have a common ancestor from which both evolved.

4. Virtually all technological advancement in human cultures has occurred in the last 40,000 years. This suggests that

    a) language may have developed quite recently within the approximately seven million year time course of human evolution.
    b) technologically advanced modern humans are a very recent occurrence in historical terms.
    c) the evolution of language in humans may have ushered in" a period of technological advancement.
    d)* all of the above

Chapter 1

5. The vocal apparatus of modern humans, as compared to that of chimpanzees, shows which of the following "speech-favoring" adaptations?

    a)   an enlarged larynx, short jaw, and compacted tooth arrangement
    b)   a more flexible jaw structure that allows a greater range of speech sounds to be made
    c)*   a rounded tongue and a voice box that is lower in the throat than that of any other species
    d)   a vocal tract with increased air flow capacity and wisdom teeth

6. The fact that modern humans have a short rounded tongue and a larynx situated lower in the throat than any other species has *primarily* been used to argue

    a)   that evolutionary adaptations have disadvantages as well as advantages.
    b)*   that a sophisticated spoken language capability developed relatively recently in human evolution.
    c)   in support of a continuity view of language evolution.
    d)   that Neanderthals were the first humans to make vowel sounds.

7. The belief that elements of language are present in other primates that share a common ancestry with humans is *most likely* to be held by

    a)*   a primatologist with a continuity view of language evolution.
    b)   a linguist with a discontinuity view of language evolution.
    c)   a cognitive psychologist who views language as a separate module in our mental system.
    d)   none of the above.

8. The view that language is a recently developed ability in humans, and one that is quite distinct from the gestures and calls of earlier hominids is the fundamental principle held by

    a)   psycholinguistic theorists.
    b)   interactive theorists.
    c)   evolutionary theorists.
    d)*   discontinuity theorists.

Copyright © Houghton Mifflin Company. All rights reserved.

9. Which of the following statements is true of the continuity and discontinuity views of language evolution?

- a) The discontinuity view maintains that language evolution is analogous to progression up a ladder, with the "bottom steps" being the gestures and calls of the hominid ancestors of modern humans.
- b)* Continuity and discontinuity views exist along a continuum and share some common ground.
- c) The discontinuity view stipulates that language and thought are not related, whereas the continuity view sees a close connection between thought and language.
- d) Continuity theorists are more likely than discontinuity theorists to view language as a separate mental module.

10. Findings of close approximations of language in nonhuman animals would support

- a) the idea that animals are more intelligent than is currently assumed.
- b) the hypothesis that speech capacity is necessary for language.
- c)* the continuity view of language evolution.
- d) all of the above.

11. If our closest living animal relatives fail to show the ability to acquire a language-like system of communication, then

- a) the continuity view is refuted.
- b) the discontinuity view is refuted.
- c)* both the continuity and discontinuity views remain viable.
- d) both the continuity and discontinuity views are refuted.

12. In comparing a word like "banana" with a word like "buzz," the one that better illustrates the arbitrariness of language is

- a)* banana.
- b) buzz.
- c) Neither demonstrates this feature better because all words are equally arbitrary.

13. The _____ character of language refers to the creativeness of human language the idea that we can continually create new words and sentences from a limited number of basic elements.

- a) semantic
- b) arbitrary
- c) discrete
- d)* productive

14. One person at a dinner table says to a second person, "Please pass the mustard." The fact that the word "mustard" has an agreed upon meaning to both individuals reflects the _____ characteristic of language.

   a)*   semantic
   b)   arbitrary
   c)   productive
   d)   discrete

15. Displacement refers to

   a)   the idea that the same concept can be expressed by several different sentences.
   b)   the discontinuity of language.
   c)*   the ability of language to communicate about the past, the absent, the future, and the imaginary.
   d)   none of the above.

16. The smallest unit of language that conveys meaning is called a

   a)   syntax.
   b)*   morpheme.
   c)   phoneme.
   d)   syllable.

17. The discreteness characteristic of language refers to

   a)*   the fact that language signals are distinct and do not vary continuously.
   b)   the ability of members of a species to understand an unspoken language signal (such as a dance or a gesture).
   c)   the fact that there are "hidden" meanings to sentences.
   d)   the universal syntactic rules, such as forming plurals by adding -S.

18. Which of Hockett's universal characteristics of language are features of language *use*?

   a)   semanticity and productivity
   b)   discreteness and arbitrariness
   c)*   productivity and displacement
   d)   arbitrariness and semanticity

19. Sign language lacks which of the universal characteristics of language?

   a)   discreteness
   b)   arbitrariness
   c)   both discreteness and arbitrariness
   d)*   none of the above

20. Which of the following natural animal communication systems shows the feature of discreteness?

    a) the dance of the honeybee
    b)* the predator calls of the vervet monkey
    c) both a) and b)
    d) none of the above

21. Which of the following natural animal communication systems shows the feature of duality of patterning?

    a) the dance of the honeybee
    b) the predator calls of the vervet monkey
    c) both a) and b)
    d)* none of the above

22. Which of the following conclusions about the attempts to teach language to nonhuman primates would be accepted by most psycholinguists?

    a)* The behavior of the trained animals shows semanticity but not productivity.
    b) The animals can learn sign language but not spoken language.
    c) Only "Kanzi" has shown evidence for true language.
    d) none of the above.

23. One of the main concerns among critics of the evidence for language learning by apes and chimps is

    a) these animals do not have enough general cognitive ability to learn a true language.
    b)* some experimenters fail to recognize when the animal is simply imitating signs to get rewards.
    c) the animals have a vocabulary of only about a dozen words or so.
    d) all of the above.

24. Cognitive psychology can be defined as:

    a) the study of the mental processes used in language.
    b)* the study of how people encode, store, and retrieve information.
    c) a scientific description of the nature of mental processes.
    d) a field that tries to describe the universal characteristics of all languages.

Chapter 1

25. The interactive view of language stresses that

    a)*   language abilities are closely intertwined with our other mental abilities.
    b)   the continuity view of language evolution must be correct.
    c)   language is just our basic cognitive ability applied to the problem of communication.
    d)   all of the above

26. As an alternative to the usual assumption that language is a tool for expressing thoughts, Whorf proposed that we are able to think only in terns of conceptual distinctions represented in our language. In other words, he said that language guides thought. This hypothesis is known as

    a)   the paradox of comprehension.
    b)*   linguistic determinism.
    c)   the modularity view.
    d)   the interactive view.

27. In Marr's scheme, the level of analysis in which we ask, "What is the system designed to accomplish?" is the

    a)*   computational level.
    b)   representational level.
    c)   implementational level.
    d)   all of the above

28. If I want to know the mental steps that expert readers use to learn new material from a text, then I am studying reading at a(n) ____ level of analysis.

    a)   computational level
    b)*   representational level
    c)   implementational level
    d)   applied

29. If I study the relationship between brain damage and the nature of the language disturbance that results from that damage, then I am studying language at a(n) ____ level of analysis.

    a)   computational level
    b)   representational level
    c)*   implementational level
    d)   applied

Copyright © Houghton Mifflin Company. All rights reserved.

30. Linguists generally operate at a(n) ____ level of analysis, while most psycholinguists work at (a) ____ level of analysis.

      a)*   computational; representational
      b)   computational; implementational
      c)   representational; implementational
      d)   algorithmic; cognitive

Integrative Essay Questions

1. Imagine that an isolated group of the genus *Homo erectus* is discovered. They seem to communicate with combinations of brief utterances, perhaps just single words, and with gestures. Which of Hockett's six features are most likely to be present? Justify your answer.

2. Let's say that you believe strongly in the discontinuity view of language evolution *and* in the interactive view of language-cognition relations. What does this suggest about the evolution of mental abilities in general? Would the current data on attempts to teach language to nonhuman primates refute this position? Why or why not?

3. If the modularity view is correct, what aspects of language are most likely to be specialized modules that operate without using general memory abilities? What aspects of language are most likely to depend more strongly on general cognitive abilities? Justify your answer.

Chapter 2
What Language Users Must Know

Keeping an Eye on the Big Picture

The most important role that the material from this chapter can play is to get the students thinking in a more sophisticated way about the questions to be addressed in the rest of the course. This chapter helps flesh out a key idea that was introduced in the first chapter, the idea that all languages have symbolic and productive aspects. However, my emphasis in Chapter 2 is to get the student to think of these aspects of language as mysteries to be solved. If they look deeply enough into each mystery they will see why at least some theorists think that language phenomena cannot be explained without reliance on the idea that some of the things we need to know are "hardwired" into the brain.

A good way to get students to see the issues in linguistics as suggesting mysteries for psycholinguists to explore is by presenting curious examples of language forms and having the students try to explain them. Several of these are used in the chapter, or you can devise ones of your own. One exercise that I have found helpful is based on Chomsky's "Colorless green ideas. . ." example. Compose a set of syntactically correct and incorrect meaningless sentences. Then pose the question of how the students know that something is wrong with certain ones if all are meaningless.

An intriguing aspect of the mystery of the productivity of language is that productivity cuts across phonology, morphology, and syntax. The chapter presents reasons to think of each of these as different kinds of knowledge, but with the same general feature of infinite productive capacity. You can anticipate this idea by asking students to come up with the longest word they know. Then add a prefix or suffix to make the word longer. Add another prefix or suffix to make the word still longer. It is worth reminding the students that productivity at more than one level is at the heart of what Hockett meant by the idea that all languages show duality of patterning, one of the six features discussed in Chapter 1.

A good exercise to introduce the mystery of meaning is to pretend to be completely naïve about particular word meanings and ask the students to try to define the terms. Then ask them to define the words they used in the definition. Keep pressing until the students see that word meanings must be somehow different from dictionary entries. Often you will find that the students come up with their own theories of meaning that have parallels to the ones discussed in the chapter.

Copyright © Houghton Mifflin Company. All rights reserved.

The Devilish Details

What's in a Grammar?

Even though the term "grammar" is familiar to the students, that familiarity can work against them. It may be difficult to get students into the habit of thinking of a grammar as a description of what a language user must know rather than as a proscriptive set of rules taught in English classes. Moreover, there may be confusion over the idea of coming up with the grammar that describes a particular language and the goal of specifying a universal grammar. Having the students compare particular grammars for both similarities and differences in how they implement the productivity of language can be a very useful exercise. The Internet is an excellent resource for this activity. For example, links to comparative grammars can be found at:

www.bucknell.edu/~rbeard/

The information available from the above site will allow students to explore the phonology and morphology of several different languages. It becomes clear quickly in comparing a few languages why a phonetic alphabet is needed and just how productive morphology can be.

Rule-based Versus Lexicalist Grammars

The various versions of Chomsky's theory can be a real struggle for students, but most of them can come to appreciate the idea of general syntactic rules and how syntactic knowledge differs from lexical and semantic knowledge. It can be frustrating for students to finally get a feel for Chomsky's ideas and then be introduced to a very different approach based on weakening some of the distinctions that Chomsky has held dear. Obviously, there is no single approach to teaching this information that is best for all students. However, I have had success with a historical approach. That is, I try to help the students see how each step in the development of modern linguistic theory made sense in the climate in which it was proposed. For example, you may want to assign Chomsky's review of Skinner's *Verbal Behavior* as outside reading. Then, discuss in class how the developments in Chomsky's own theory represent his attempts to address the issues that he said behavioral approaches could not address. Finally, contrast Chomsky's assumptions with those of lexical functionalist grammar. If you wish to have the students further explore lexicalist grammars, a good Internet resource can be found at the following:

www.sil.org/linguistics/

Nature Versus Nurture is an Issue for Syntax *and* for Semantics

Students often have trouble seeing what could be innate about language when it seems so obvious that a language is learned. Accordingly, it is important to point out that in Chomsky's latest theory the principles (like uniqueness) and parameters (like the head parameter) provide an innate foundation for making acquisition manageable. It is at least arguable that there is just too much to be learned too fast without having some kind of basic blueprint. It may be more difficult for the

Chapter 2

students to see this same issue with regard to meaning. One way to help the students see that there is a legitimate question regarding innateness in semantics is to build on the introductory exercise that I suggested above in which you have the students try to break out of the circularity of definitions. For each of the three views of meaning discussed in the chapter, you can ask how a particular word could be defined and see how far you can keep breaking down those meanings. Then ask, "Where would these 'atoms' of meaning come from?"

Multiple Choice Test Items

1. Which of the following demonstrates tacit knowledge?

    a) You know things about yourself that no one else knows.
    b)* You look at two possible spellings of a word and pick one just because "it looks right."
    c) You look at two possible spellings of a word and pick one because it follows a spelling rule like "I before e."
    d) all of the above

2. You know that to form a word that expresses the opposite of *exciting*, you can add *un-* to the beginning of the word and produce *unexciting*. This example demonstrates knowledge of

    a) phonology.
    b)* morphology.
    c) syntax.
    d) semantics.

3. Knowing when to produce an aspirated /t/ and when to produce one that is unaspirated is an example of knowledge of

    a)* phonology.
    b) morphology.
    c) syntax.
    d) semantics.

4. Which of the following best expresses the relationship between an allophone and a phoneme?

    a) Phonemes and allophones are two different kinds of basic speech sounds.
    b) Phonemes are elements of phonology and allophones are elements of morphology.
    c) Allophones have meaning but phonemes do not.
    d)* Phonemes are categories of different allophones.

Copyright © Houghton Mifflin Company. All rights reserved.

5. Consonant phonemes vary in terms of

    a)   voicing.
    b)   point of articulation.
    c)   manner of articulation.
    d)* all of the above.

6. If you say the phrase "tough stains," the difference in the two /t/ sounds is that the first is ____ and the second is _____.

    a)   an allophone; a phoneme
    b)   a stop; a fricative
    c)   a fricative; a stop
    d)* aspirated; unaspirated

7. Stop, fricative, and nasal are examples of different

    a)   allophones.
    b)   phonemes.
    c)   points of articulation.
    d)* manners of articulation.

8. Bilabial, alveolar, and palatal are examples of different

    a)   phonemes.
    b)* points of articulation.
    c)   manners of articulation.
    d)   none of the above

9. Vowel sounds vary based on

    a)* the position of the tongue.
    b)   the degree to which the teeth are used to block the flow of air.
    c)   the degree of voicing of the sound.
    d)   all of the above.

10. You can easily tell that "florg" could be an English word but "gfrol" could not. The knowledge that allows you to make these decisions is your knowledge of

    a)* sequence constraints.
    b)   assimilation rules.
    c)   correspondence rules.
    d)   pragmatics.

Chapter 2   15

11. In English, people appear to follow a rule that we aspirate the consonant before a vowel at the beginning of a word. This rule

    a)   shows that pronunciation of consonants varies by the context in which they occur.
    b)   is obeyed unconsciously by the speaker.
    c)   can be considered to be tacit phonological knowledge.
    d)*   all of the above

12. The process of altering a sound to make it and the adjacent sound easier to produce together is known as

    a)   an inflection rule.
    b)*   assimilation.
    c)   a sequence constraint.
    d)   a glide pronunciation.

13. Adding –s to make a noun plural is one of the _____ rules of English.

    a)   phonological
    b)   sequence
    c)*   inflection
    d)   derivational

14. We can change a verb to an adverb with the addition of the suffix –ly, as in love +ly →lovely. This is an example of one of the ____ rules of English.

    a)   phonological
    b)   sequence
    c)   inflection
    d)*   derivational

15. The word *lovely* is composed of two morphemes, *love,* which is a ____ morpheme, and *–ly*, which is a ____ morpheme.

    a)*   free; bound
    b)   bound; free
    c)   inflectional; derivational
    d)   derivational; inflectional

16. If we examine the morphology of a given language through time, we see that

    a)   there are major historical changes.
    b)   it is marked by the creation of many new forms.
    c)   it is governed by general rules.
    d)*   all of the above

Copyright © Houghton Mifflin Company. All rights reserved.

17. If a child learns that the past tense of *go* is *went*, and the child then stops using *goed*, the child may have applied the _____ principle of morphology.

    a) derivational
    b) transformational
    c)* uniqueness
    d) productivity

18. According to Pinker (1990), the uniqueness principle may be one example of

    a)* an innate aspect of morphology.
    b) an innate aspect of syntax.
    c) a learned aspect of morphology.
    d) a learned aspect of syntax.

19. If I keep making a sentence longer and longer by adding a new phrase on to the end of the sentence, I have shown that language has ____

    a) a capacity for iteration.
    b) infinite productivity.
    c) syntactic rules for combining words.
    d)* all of the above.

20. I can create a new sentence by embedding a new clause inside a particular sentence. By adding another clause inside the new sentence, I have

    a) violated a morphological rule.
    b) violated a syntactic rule.
    c) demonstrated iteration.
    d)* demonstrated recursion.

21. In a simple finite state grammar (FSG), the third word generated in a sentence depends upon

    a) phrase structure rules.
    b)* the preceding word in the sentence.
    c) transitional rules of performance.
    d) all of the above.

22. One way that Chomsky's view of linguistics differs from Bloomfield's view is that Chomsky is mainly interested in describing

    a) the mental processes involved in language performance.
    b)* the tacit knowledge that is required for language competence.
    c) how children learn to understand and produce language.
    d) all of the above.

Chapter 2
17

23. A theory of grammar that specified what utterances are legal and how these utterances are related to each other but which could not possibly be the basis for natural language acquisition would have _____ adequacy but not _____ adequacy.

    a)   explanatory; descriptive
    b)*   descriptive; explanatory
    c)   performance; competence
    d)   competence; performance

24. In Chomsky's theory of transformational grammar, the role of transformations is to

    a)   move elements within phrase structures.
    b)   delete elements from within phrase structures.
    c)   add elements to phrase structures.
    d)*   all of the above

25. In Chomsky's theory of transformational grammar, the same sentence could have two completely different interpretations if the same ___ structure could be mapped onto two different ___ structures.

    a)   phrase; semantic
    b)   phrase; deep
    c)   deep; surface
    d)*   surface; deep

26. In Chomsky's theory of transformational grammar, the term *deep structure* was equivalent to

    a)   meaning.
    b)   the phrase structure.
    c)   the semantic component.
    d)*   none of the above.

27. Which of the following is true regarding Chomsky's newest theory of grammar, the principles and parameters theory?

    a)   There is only one kind of transformation.
    b)   There are still two types of phrase structures.
    c)   The changes from the old theory were motivated by concerns about explanatory adequacy.
    d)*   all of the above

Copyright © Houghton Mifflin Company. All rights reserved.

28. In X-bar phrase analysis, each phrase has a head that determines what kind of phrase it is. According to Chomsky, part of your innate knowledge about language is your tacit understanding that all phrases in a language have their heads in the same position. This is known as the

    a)   alpha parameter.
    b)   uniqueness principle.
    c)   head principle.
    d)*   head parameter.

29. An important difference between Chomsky's theory of transformational grammar and his newer principles and parameters theory is that the more recent theory

    a)   states rules in a less abstract fashion.
    b)   uses only one kind of phrase structure.
    c)*   is more specific regarding what aspects of grammar may be innate.
    d)   all of the above

30. In contrast to Chomsky's ideas of grammar, proponents of lexicalist grammars argue that there is no need to rely on the concept of ____ to explain syntax because the necessary information could be stored in the lexicon.

    a)   phrase structure rules
    b)*   transformations
    c)   innate knowledge
    d)   all of the above

31. Understanding what a particular word means is the issue of ____, while understanding what a sentence means as a whole is the issue of ____.

    a)*   lexical semantics; compositional semantics
    b)   compositional semantics; lexical semantics
    c)   lexical grammar; pragmatics
    d)   semantics; synonymy

32. Charlene is graduating from medical school, and she is asked to give a speech because she is the highest ranking student, or valedictorian. In this situation, the reference for valedictorian is

    a)*   Charlene.
    b)   highest ranking student.
    c)   both a) and b).

Chapter 2   19

33. Charlene is graduating from medical school, and she is asked to give a speech because she is the highest ranking student, or valedictorian. In this situation, the sense of valedictorian is

      a)   Charlene.
      b)*   highest ranking student.
      c)   both a) and b).

34. A relationship between concepts that can, in principle, be true or false is known as a(n)

      a)   mental model.
      b)   entailment.
      c)   semantic primitive.
      d)*   proposition.

35. Which view defines meaning in terms of a logical relationship between an utterance and states of affairs in possible worlds?

      a)*   truth-conditional semantics
      b)   conceptual semantics
      c)   cognitive grammar
      d)   none of the above

36. Which view defines meaning completely in terms of innate semantic knowledge?

      a)   truth-conditional semantics
      b)   conceptual semantics
      c)   cognitive grammar
      d)*   none of the above

37. Which view considers semantic decomposition to be a fundamental part of lexical semantics?

      a)   truth-conditional semantics
      b)*   conceptual semantics
      c)   cognitive grammar
      d)   all of the above

38. Which view considers mental models of situations in the world to be fundamental to explaining meaning?

      a)   truth-conditional semantics
      b)   conceptual semantics
      c)*   cognitive grammar
      d)   all of the above

Copyright © Houghton Mifflin Company. All rights reserved.

39. Which one of the following features of the concept *dog* is most likely to be considered a semantic primitive?

    a)   barks
    b)   is a pet
    c)*   is animate
    d)   all of the above

40. Which of the following represents the basic level of abstraction?

    a)   living thing
    b)   animal
    c)*   fish
    d)   goldfish

Integrative Essay Questions

1. Is it possible to point to any particular word and identify it as the longest word in the English language? Explain. What does your answer say about the productivity of phonology? Of morphology?

2. Discuss the problems with finite state grammars. Be clear as to how they fail both in descriptive adequacy and in explanatory adequacy. In what way did Chomsky's transformational grammar provide a better description of language competence? How does his latest theory better address the explanatory adequacy criterion?

3. Draw a phrase structure tree for the following sentence:

    George stayed after school with the teacher.

Now extend the tree one level further by showing the morphemes that compose each word (where there is more than one in a given word). Should this tree diagram be considered as one kind of knowledge or as two (syntactic and morphemic)? Explain.

4. Using the sentence you diagrammed in the previous question, compare and contrast how the meaning of the sentence would be explained in conceptual semantics and in cognitive grammar. Which one of the two views of meaning maintains the stronger distinction between syntax and semantics?

5. Summarize the claims made by linguists who believe that explaining both the productivity and the meaning of language requires some innate endowments? Which of the claims seem strongest to you? Which appear weakest? Justify your choices.

Chapter 3
Language in Relation to Other Cognitive Processes

Keeping an Eye on the Big Picture

This chapter helps to further build a foundation for addressing a question that runs throughout the whole book: When we study the processes involved in language, are we studying one mental faculty among many or are we studying a general mental ability applied to the goal of communication? Of course, it turns out that language processes are both "special" and highly integrated with the rest of cognition. So that students can appreciate this conclusion later, this chapter provides an overview of the cognitive processes that will be most intimately tied to language in the upcoming chapters.

Because the question of the independence of language as a mental process can be asked at both the representational and implementational levels of analysis, this chapter also affords the opportunity for students to think about the relationship between the cognitive and physiological contexts of language. If the students have not previously had a course in cognitive psychology, they may still be having difficulty seeing how one can study mental processes apart from studying the brain or how having a functional theory of mental processes can guide brain research. You may want to start with an exercise like the following one, which I have used a number of times to good effect.

Have the students imagine that they want to determine which of two study strategies, rereading a text chapter several times or using the PQ4R strategy (discussed in most introductory psychology texts), is most effective. You can point out that it is relatively straightforward to equate total study time between the two conditions. After discussing how to test this question, I have the students make predictions about whether one strategy will prove better than another and *why*. The *why* question will not only inform you about their current knowledge and beliefs about memory but also gives you a chance to point out that the explanation for the greater effectiveness of one strategy can be cast completely at a mental-processes level without any reference to brain events. You can then point out that knowing the explanation behind the effectiveness of a particular strategy could guide research on where particular processes are localized in the brain. An added bonus: if you also present a few of the available studies on the effectiveness of a system like PQ4R, you may get some of the students to improve their study skills! Finally, when students finish the discussion of memory in the chapter, you can tie in what they have learned with this introductory exercise by having them explain why PQ4R works using concepts from basic memory research.

Copyright © Houghton Mifflin Company. All rights reserved.

The Devilish Details

The DTC and the Development of Cognitive Psychology

You may find it useful to spend a bit of time on the experiments that tried to test the derivational theory of complexity. These are cogently summarized in Fodor, Bever, and Garrett (1974). In my view, the point of such an exercise is to make clear a general point that many students do not grasp easily: a theory does not have to be "correct" to be useful. It is not hard to show that even though the DTC proved hard to test as transformational grammar changed and was interpreted differently by various linguists and psychologists, the research by George Miller and by Jerry Fodor that tried to test the theory led the way to further studies of both sentence memory and sentence processing time. In fact, the continuing influence of their work is clearly reflected in much of the research that is presented in Chapter 7 of the text.

From Short-Term to Working Memory

One of the more important trends in memory research, at least in terms of the implications for language processing, has been how the concept of short-term memory has changed from a simple storage buffer to a mental workspace. The newer conceptions of working memory blur the lines between attention and memory, so it may be useful to help the students see how the standard model of short-term and long-term memory has undergone revision as people tried to determine the role of short-term memory storage in paradigms beyond list learning. Activity 3.2 in the text asks the students to try out a task that Baddeley and Hitch (1974) used to make this very point: manipulation of information in short-term storage is involved in many kinds of language, memory, and reasoning tasks. Other tasks used to show the effects of WM loads on cognitive performance are easy to simulate in class. For example, you can pace the students through a passage by presenting one sentence at a time on an overhead projector. In one condition, the students get a single passage, but in another condition the sentences alternate between two passages as in the following:

> The coal miner's strike was getting ugly.
> The power of computers has increased over the years even as their size has been reduced.
> The workers felt that the managers were "bean counters" with little understanding of the risks of mining.
> The first computers were room-sized behemoths with less power than the desktop models of today.

Continue this for several sentences from each passage. Then, discuss with the students what kinds of problems the interleaved passages presented for them. It should be clear that we need attentional capacity to understand a given sentence and that we have to hold some information from a previous sentence to keep a coherent idea of what a text is saying. Clearly, there is more to this than just having seven "slots" to hold information in a passive buffer. This discussion can be related not only to the concept of working memory in this chapter but also to Chapter 8 on discourse comprehension.

Copyright © Houghton Mifflin Company. All rights reserved.

Chapter 3

Priming and Automaticity

Priming techniques are used so often as a tool in psycholinguistics that it is important that students understand the basic ideas behind the phenomenon. Spreading activation and semantic distance are appealing metaphors (perhaps too appealing in that they are sometimes taken literally), so students tend not to have great difficulty with these ideas. More problematic is how researchers know that priming can be automatic. The automaticity of priming is nicely illustrated by Neely's (1977) work, which is why I highlighted that research in the chapter. However, the subtleties of this work can be difficult for the students.

I like to use an exercise in which I ask the students to imagine how Neely's study could be adapted to test the hypotheses of two researchers. I tell them that one researcher thinks that poor readers have a slower spread of activation in their semantic networks. The other researcher thinks that poor readers have normal speed of spreading activation but that these readers cannot use conscious expectations as well as good readers. By working through how the data would look in each condition for each hypothesis, the students come to see how the SOA and shift manipulations were used to show what is and is not automatic.

Interactive and Modular Processing

Many of the psycholinguistic experiments that the students will learn about in upcoming chapters were devised to address the relative contribution of bottom-up and top-down processes to some aspect of language performance. Unfortunately, students often struggle with the concepts of top-down and bottom-up processing. It is possible to help them by creating a simple network in class, with students as the nodes. You can pattern the exercise after Figure 3.12 and divide the students into levels, with the top level knowing what patterns could be presented (either of two words, for example). Then show features of letters to one level and let them communicate with the next level, and so on until the people at the top level know what the word is. Now add top-down processing. Present a few visual features that rule out some letter possibilities and allow the word level to tell the letter level what to look for. Note how this could be advantageous if the feature information is becoming available over time (as though the visual feature comes gradually into focus).

This exercise can serve as the basis for clarifying other concepts as well. Discuss with the class how you could change each level so that it was a distributed representation. Then talk about how processing would change if units (people) were removed from the network, analogous to a brain lesion. This idea leads naturally into relating interactive and modular notions to neuropsychology.

Copyright © Houghton Mifflin Company. All rights reserved.

Multiple Choice Test Items

1. When Wundt established the first psychology laboratory in 1879, his intent was to use ____ to understand the basic elements of conscious experience.

    a) S-R theory
    b)* introspection
    c) visual imagery
    d) paired associate learning

2. An important aspect of Chomsky's view of language that influenced psychologists was the idea that

    a) language processing is one aspect of our general mental abilities.
    b)* the explanation for language phenomena should not be restricted to studying observable behavior.
    c) language could be explained based on observable behavior.
    d) none of the above

3. One of the earliest goals in modern psycholinguistics was to determine the viability of Chomsky's transformational grammar as a model of language performance. The idea that the transformations in Chomsky's theory reflected the actual mental processes in comprehension was known as

    a) the standard model.
    b)* the derivational theory of complexity.
    c) the procedural theory of syntax.
    d) Chomskyan psycholinguistics.

4. The "magic number seven" that George Miller referred to in his classic paper represented

    a) a fundamental limitation on our information processing capacity.
    b) the number of chunks of information most people could remember in an immediate memory test.
    c) support for the distinction between STM and LTM.
    d)* all of the above.

5. A researcher who studies associative learning of nonsense syllables would most likely be

    a)* a behaviorist interested in basic aspects of human learning.
    b) a psycholinguist testing the derivational theory of complexity.
    c) a cognitive psychologist studying the capacity of STM.
    d) a linguist examining basic aspects of language acquisition.

Chapter 3

6. Some cognitive psychologists think of the distinction between computer hardware and software as analogous to the distinction between

   a)   linguistics and psycholinguistics.
   b)   psycholinguistics and linguistics.
   c)* brain and mind.
   d)   mind and brain.

7. Compared to the 1950s and early 1960s, the late 1960s and 1970s marked a period in which cognitive psychology

   a)   made increasing strides to integrate linguistics and psychology.
   b)   viewed language as a special ability separate from our general information processing abilities.
   c)* de-emphasized linguistic theory in the study of the mental processes in language.
   d)   none of the above

8. In the multistore model of memory proposed by Atkinson and Shiffrin (1968), recoding information in a speech format would take place in the

   a)   sensory register.
   b)* short-term store.
   c)   long-term store.
   d)   all of the above.

9. When some asks, "What did you do last night?" and the movie you watched comes to mind, the information about the movie just underwent

   a)   sensory registration.
   b)   semantic coding.
   c)   short-term memory scanning.
   d)* retrieval from long-term memory.

10. Bransford and Franks (1971) showed that long-term memory for sentences tended to capture the gist of the sentence and that the gist was often elaborated based on world knowledge. This finding suggests that

   a)   there are close ties between language processes and memory processes.
   b)   long-term memory for sentences seldom involves retention of the surface structure.
   c)   sentence comprehension may be a constructive process.
   d)* all of the above

Copyright © Houghton Mifflin Company. All rights reserved.

11. A major difference between the concept of "working memory" and the concept of the "short-term store" is that working memory

    a)   holds speech codes.
    b)*   consists of more than one kind of buffer.
    c)   is not as limited in capacity as the short-term store.
    d)   all of the above

12. If you gave someone an articulatory suppression task while the person tried to do a verbal reasoning problem, you would be testing for the role of the _____ in verbal reasoning.

    a)*   phonological loop
    b)   visual-spatial sketch pad
    c)   the central executive
    d)   all of the above

13. The "central executive" in Baddeley's model of working memory is best thought of as

    a)   what was referred to in the multistore model as control processes.
    b)   short-term memory.
    c)   the active portion of long-term memory.
    d)*   a system for allocating our limited attentional resources.

14. A major reason that people may perform poorly on reasoning problems, such as syllogisms, is that

    a)*   working memory limitations make it difficult to manipulate more than one model of the problem.
    b)   on verbal problems, people tend to use their visual-spatial sketch pad when they should use their phonological loop.
    c)   they fail to retrieve the correct answer from long-term memory.
    d)   all of the above

15. Declarative memory is to ___ as procedural memory is to ____.

    a)   general knowledge; personal experience
    b)*   facts; skills
    c)   semantic information; episodic information
    d)   episodic information; semantic information

Chapter 3   27

16. Compared to information retrieved in a controlled fashion, information retrieved in an automatic fashion

      a)*   can be detected at shorter stimulus onset asynchronies (SOAs).
      b)   involves inhibition but not facilitation.
      c)   depends on the retrieval strategy being used.
      d)   all of the above

17. In a lexical decision experiment, response time to the word "chair" would be speeded by preceding it with the word "furniture." The word "carpet" might be speeded by preceding it with "furniture" but the effect would be smaller than that for "chair." This illustrates

      a)   a typicality effect.
      b)   an automatic process.
      c)   spreading activation.
      d)*   all of the above.

18. In Bartlett's (1932) experiment in which English people tried to recall a Native American folktale,

      a)*   the people interpreted and recalled the story from the standpoint of their own world views.
      b)   memory was poor because there was no opportunity for spreading activation to work.
      c)   memory for the story was excellent because it was meaningful, unlike a set of nonsense syllables.
      d)   people could not recall the story but they could recognize it.

19. Of the following, which is the best example of a schema?

      a)*   your knowledge of what takes place at a dentist's office
      b)   the knowledge of chemistry someone has after an introductory course
      c)   the knowledge of chemistry that a chemist has
      d)   a mental image of a friend's face

20. Several studies, including the seminal work of Hyde and Jenkins (1969), showed that the way stimuli were encoded is more important to memory than intent to commit the stimuli to memory. This finding supports the

      a)   multistore model of memory.
      b)   spreading activation theory of memory.
      c)*   levels of processing theory.
      d)   none of the above

Copyright © Houghton Mifflin Company. All rights reserved.

21. Elaborative processing of information can help memory by

   a)   forcing you to repeat a stimulus more often in short-term memory.
   b)* making more connections that could serve as retrieval routes.
   c)   processing a stimulus to a deeper level.
   d)   preventing information from decaying.

22. The fan effect shows that

   a)   elaboration makes memory retrieval easier.
   b)   interference effects are found in recall but not in recognition.
   c)   decay affects recognition, whereas interference affects recall.
   d)* none of the above.

23. If you memorize a set of sentences, it seems as though the information is stored as a network of propositions. If the propositions do not form a schema, then the more links off of a concept

   a)   the faster the retrieval of the information.
   b)* the slower the retrieval of the information.
   c)   the more automatic the spread of activation.
   d)   none of the above.

24. The idea that the memorability of a stimulus depends on the similarity of the encoding and retrieval contexts is known as

   a)* the encoding specificity principle.
   b)   levels of processing theory.
   c)   the fan effect.
   d)   the interference theory of forgetting.

25. If you are reading a poem in order to memorize it, you would probably read differently than if you were reading in order to interpret the poem. Such encoding of information in the way that best fits how you will be asked to remember it is known as

   a)   the fan effect.
   b)   elaborative processing.
   c)* transfer-appropriate processing.
   d)   associative learning.

26. During the cognitive stage of skill acquisition, you

   a)   learn to smoothly coordinate the different parts of the skill.
   b)   come to perform the skill automatically.
   c)* use a declarative representation of the skill.
   d)   abandon a procedural representation of the skill.

Chapter 3

27. During the autonomous stage of skill acquisition, you

    a)   establish a procedural representation for the first time.
    b)   come to perform the skill as well as you will ever perform it.
    c)   analyze the skill in terms of production rules.
    d)*   none of the above

28. Propositions are to ___ as production rules are to ___.

    a)   theories; facts
    b)   cognitive models; neural models
    c)*   declarative knowledge; procedural knowledge
    d)   all of the above

29. Which of the following is true regarding the nature of parallel distributed processing (PDP) models?

    a)*   None of the individual units in a PDP model actually store information.
    b)   Different layers of units are used as descriptions of different kinds of neurons.
    c)   Such models focus on performance of a process, rather than its acquisition.
    d)   all of the above.

30. The connectionist model of word recognition developed by McClelland and Rumelhart (1981) explains word recognition in terms of

    a)   the bottom-up flow of activation from features to letters to words.
    b)   neurons located in a particular region of the brain.
    c)   a series of production rules.
    d)*   the interaction of top-down and bottom-up processes in a network.

31. According to Fodor's (1983) idea of the modularity of the mind, an example of an input system with a modular architecture is

    a)   memory.
    b)*   language.
    c)   perception.
    d)   all of the above

32. Fodor (1983) argued that our mental modules are informationally encapsulated. What he means by this claim is that

    a)*   the flow of information is bottom-up only.
    b)   a module works with only one kind of information.
    c)   each module is localized to a particular brain region.
    d)   a module can only send information to other modules, not to the central system.

Copyright © Houghton Mifflin Company. All rights reserved.

33. If, in Fodor's terms, we have a module for syntactic processing, then syntactic processing

   a)* occurs in one particular region of the brain.
   b) is possible only after semantic processing of a sentence takes place.
   c) is based on conceptually driven processes.
   d) all of the above

34. One thing that connectionist and modular theories have in common is that they

   a) agree that language processing is bottom-up.
   b)* try to make it easier to integrate representational and implementational levels of analysis .
   c) agree on the distinction between input systems and the central system.
   d) do away with the idea of procedural knowledge.

Integrative Essay Questions

1. Draw a diagram with a timeline on the x-axis and the degree of integration of linguistics into psychology on the y-axis. Draw in a line that shows the relationship between linguistics and psychology in the 1950s, 1960s, 1970s, 1980s, and 1990s. For each major shift in direction, point out whose work in linguistics or psychology was influential in changing the degree of integration.

2. Let's say that you replicated Neely's (1977) experiment on semantic priming of lexical decisions, except that you had a group of people who had brain damage that affected their ability to perform a controlled shift of attention. Describe what aspects of the data would be the same as Neely's and what aspects would differ.

3. Describe the basic components of Baddeley's (1986) model of working memory. What role might each component play in your comprehension of a sentence such as, "The chair is to the right of the table, which is in the center of the room"? Why and how would comprehension break down if more and more items were added to the spatial description?

4. In English, we typically form the past tense of a verb by adding –*ed*. How would the representation of this rule in memory differ depending on whether it is a declarative or procedural knowledge structure? How might the representation for this rule exist in a PDP network?

Copyright © Houghton Mifflin Company. All rights reserved.

Chapter 4
Theories of the Language-Thought Relationship

Keeping an Eye on the Big Picture

The primary goal of this final chapter of the first unit of the text is to complete the job of laying the groundwork for the consideration of the relationship between language and other cognitive processes. In addition, this material also affords the opportunity to place the study of language into a social context. However, to accomplish these ends, I wanted to avoid the typical presentation of ideas on the language-thought relationship as the simple question of whether Whorf was right or wrong. I believe there is much more for students to learn about the idea that language may play a guiding role in thinking than the notion that Whorf's ideas were an interesting, but ultimately pointless, cul-de-sac in the history of psycholinguistics.

A useful way to form a bridge between the material in the last couple of chapters and the current chapter is to consider the problem of translating from one language to another. For example, with the background they now have, you can remind students of the story in Chapter 2 about the computer translator's difficulty with the idiom "The spirit is willing but the flesh is weak." Based on the information in Chapter 2, the students should be able to discuss the problems such a translation system would have if it tried to work on a word-by-word basis. In fact, some of the earliest translators did work on a word-by-word basis, and some low-cost systems are available now that still work this way. The students should be able to discuss what limitations they would expect to see in these systems. You can review earlier material by asking what information the automated translator system would have to have in order to work better than a word-by-word system allows. Then, ask the students to imagine that you have a system that has substantial information about the syntax and semantics of the languages it is supposed to translate. What problems could still arise? It might help to work with an extreme case, such as trying to translate from the language of a stone-age culture to a modern one and vice versa. Clearly, there will be terms in one language for which there is no corresponding term in the other language. You can then introduce linguistic determinism in this context as perhaps the ultimate stumbling block to translators, one that goes beyond the lack of correspondence between terms to the very issue of whether two cultures with two different languages *are capable* of understanding the world in the same way.

The Devilish Details

The Difference Between Relativity and Determinism

It is sometimes difficult for students to appreciate the difference between the correlational hypothesis, linguistic relativity, and the causal hypothesis, linguistic determinism. It may be helpful for them to see the differences in the implications of each hypothesis for the problem of whether two different cultures can learn to really understand each other. A relevant project that many students find useful and interesting can be pursued as a follow-up to the introductory discussion I suggested above. Specifically, you can give students an assignment to find out how some commercial translation systems actually work. General descriptions of the algorithms the systems use can be found in a number of places, including on the Internet. Then, as the material in this chapter is covered, students can consider whether potential examples of linguistic determinism or linguistic relativity would impact on the efficiency of the translation algorithm.

What Constitutes Evidence for Language Influencing Thought?

Because language is a tool for expressing thoughts, there is a fine, but important, distinction between the influence of the thoughts behind a sentence on someone else's thoughts and the effect of language itself on thinking. Some phenomena that students (and some psychologists!) believe illustrate the effect of language on cognition may only represent a case where language was used to communicate an influential idea. This point can be difficult to appreciate, but it also is an opportunity for students to get some practice at thinking about how to get evidence for cause and effect relationships. For example, as I pointed out in the chapter, even though several of the classic studies of the effects of verbal labels on memory are sometimes interpreted within a linguistic determinism framework, the data need not be viewed as language effects per se. If you want to bring in an example from outside the text, you might have students consider some of the classic demonstrations of perceptual set. For example, the ambiguous figure that can be seen as an old or young woman, ubiquitous in introductory psychology texts, is quite subject to perceptual set. You can have the students identify what is in the picture after reading them either a brief story about a young lady or an old woman. Have the students interpret how this effect fits into the linguistic determinism hypothesis. Then ask them if they might get the same effect from imagining an old woman rather than hearing a story.

It is worthwhile to point out that what linguistic determinism predicts is that *differing forms* of a linguistic expression have different effects on thinking, even though the two forms may be logically equivalent. This type of evidence avoids some of the interpretive problems revealed by the exercise on perceptual set. The students may be able to suggest several "real life" examples of framing effects that seem in line with at least a weak version of linguistic determinism.

The Concept of Bidirectional Effects

Knowing how to determine whether one variable causes a change in another is an important step for students to take, but it is still another matter to appreciate that two factors can mutually influence each other. This, of course, is the point behind the material on the linguistic intergroup bias. The biased use of language does not, by itself, create in-groups and out-groups, but group ties may be strengthened or weakened by how the groups use language. You might want to expand on this issue by discussing how racist language is used to support prejudice. There are a large number of sources for examples of racist discourse that can be analyzed in class. I especially recommend the work by Teun van Dijk (1984, 1987, 1997) in this area.

Multiple Choice Test Items

1. Which one of the following believed that speech and thought were one and the same?

    a)   Aristotle
    b)   Lev Vygotsky
    c)* John Watson
    d)   Scott Smith

2. According to the developmental psychologist Lev Vygotsky, children's speech plays a central role in ___ before it plays a major role in ___.

    a)* thinking; communication with others
    b)   communication with others; thinking
    c)   behavior; thinking
    d)   thinking; behavior

3. The idea that linguistic differences between languages are correlated with cultural variations in ways of thinking is known as

    a)   the Sapir-Whorf hypothesis.
    b)   linguistic determinism.
    c)* linguistic relativity.
    d)   the Vygotsky-Allport hypothesis.

4. The notion that our language has a causal influence on the way that we think is known as

    a)   the Sapir-Whorf hypothesis.
    b)* linguistic determinism.
    c)   linguistic relativity.
    d)   the Vygotsky-Allport hypothesis.

5. The central idea behind the Sapir-Whorf hypothesis was that primitive cultures stay primitive because of their primitive languages.

    a)   true
    b)* false

Copyright © Houghton Mifflin Company. All rights reserved.

6. Whorf's famous example that Eskimos recognize different types of snow because they have many different words for snow

    a)   was based on a misunderstanding of differences among Arctic peoples.
    b)   is not considered a valid argument for linguistic determinism.
    c)   was not considered by Whorf himself to be the most important evidence for his hypothesis.
    d)*   all of the above

7. Documenting the existence of differences in language and patterns of thoughts between two cultures is more relevant to tests of linguistic relativity than to tests of linguistic determinism.

    a)*   true
    b)   false

8. The finding by Berlin and Kay (1969) that across cultures there is a very regular pattern to which colors are given distinct names suggests that

    a)*   there are universal perceptual principles behind color naming.
    b)   color naming practices support the Sapir-Whorf hypothesis.
    c)   color naming practices support the linguistic relativity hypothesis.
    d)   all of the above

9. Heider (1972) found that the members of the Dani tribe

    a)   perceived colors differently from other groups who have more distinct color names in their language.
    b)*   perceived colors similarly to other groups who have more distinct color names in their language.
    c)   perceived easily coded colors better than less easily coded colors.
    d)   named as many colors as other groups, contrary to Whorf's claims.

10. Which of the following words best exemplifies Zipf's law?

    a)   computer
    b)*   can
    c)   ergo
    d)   fey

Chapter 4

11. Overall, studies of the relationship between color names in a language and the processing of information about color suggest that

    a)   linguistic determinism cannot be tested using color naming and color processing.
    b)   color perception and color memory are universals, so there is no cultural variation in these processes.
    c)*   color naming practices may affect memory for color, but not basic color perception.
    d)   color naming practices are strongly related to color perception.

12. It is easier for children to learn to count in Chinese than in English or French because in Chinese

    a)*   number names follow a more regular pattern that makes place value clear.
    b)   the system of number names follows Zipf's law.
    c)   there are only names for *one, two,* and *many.*
    d)   none of the above

13. Counterfactual reasoning refers to the ability to

    a)   rebut someone else's argument.
    b)*   consider hypotheses that you know are contrary to fact.
    c)   use language to recognize fallacies in your own reasoning.
    d)   all of the above

14. Bloom (1981) argued that because Chinese lacks an explicit form for marking counterfactuals, speakers of Chinese have more difficulty with counterfactual reasoning. His claim

    a)   remains controversial.
    b)   may represent an important type of linguistic determinism.
    c)   may reflect the difficulty of performing studies of reasoning that depend on translating the same materials across two languages.
    d)*   all of the above

15. Hoffman, Lau, and Johnson (1986) found that social judgments were more often based on stereotypes when

    a)*   some of the person's traits matched up with a stereotype that was easily coded within a language.
    b)   bilinguals were exposed to descriptions in two languages.
    c)   personality descriptions were presented in English rather than in Chinese.
    d)   personality descriptions were presented in Chinese rather than in English.

Copyright © Houghton Mifflin Company. All rights reserved.

16. What conclusion can be drawn from classic studies, such as Bartlett's, (1932), which show that people's memory for a visual stimulus appears to be influenced by the verbal label for the stimulus?

    a)   Memory, more than color perception, is subject to linguistic determinism.
    b)*   Memories are subject to distortion from other information after a delay.
    c)   Whorf's ideas were a rediscovery of principles already established by early memory investigators.
    d)   all of the above

17. What conclusion can be drawn from research by Loftus and colleagues on the relationship between leading questions and eyewitness testimony?

    a)   Information provided within a question can influence later reports of what an eyewitness actually saw.
    b)   The linguistic form of a question, such as using a definite or indefinite article, can influence memory reconstruction.
    c)   People sometimes report "facts" that are inconsistent with what they actually saw.
    d)*   all of the above

18. Even if two problems are logically equivalent, people will often choose different solutions depending on whether the options are stated in terms of gains or losses. This phenomenon is known as a(n)

    a)   intergroup bias.
    b)   relativity effect.
    c)   linguistic bias.
    d)*   framing effect.

19. The framing effect shows that

    a)   linguistic relativity holds for reasoning but not perception.
    b)   reasoning shows linguistic relativity but not linguistic determinism.
    c)*   language effects on reasoning demonstrate a weak form of linguistic determinism.
    d)   none of the above.

20. People tend to be more willing to take risks when the options to resolve a problem are considered in terms of what

    a)   will be gained with each option.
    b)*   will be lost with each option.
    c)   has been tried before.
    d)   one's peer group may think of the solution.

Chapter 4

21. On which kind of problem may verbalizing your thoughts be detrimental to finding a solution?

    a)   A problem that has many elements that are difficult to remember.
    b)*   A problem in which the solution tends to come quite suddenly.
    c)   Any problem that is presented verbally rather than pictorially.
    d)   Any problem that is presented pictorially rather than verbally.

22. What conclusion can be drawn from research on the effects of masculine terms to refer to people in general, such as the use of *policeman* rather than *police officer*?

    a)   There is some evidence that sexist language influences thought in subtle ways.
    b)   More data are needed in order to determine the extent to which such usage influences attitudes.
    c)   There is no solid evidence that such sexist language affects overt behaviors such as the career choices that young women make.
    d)*   all of the above

23. According to the _____, the same overt behavior can be described at different levels of abstraction.

    a)*   linguistic category model
    b)   framing effect
    c)   linguistic intergroup bias
    d)   Sapir-Whorf hypothesis

24. Your best friend and your worst enemy are both caught shoplifting. For which person are you likely to describe their action at the highest level of abstraction in the linguistic category model?

    a)   your friend
    b)*   your enemy
    c)   Neither—negative behaviors tend to be described as action verbs.

25. Based on the linguistic intergroup bias, you would predict that someone would describe the positive behaviors by members of a rival sports team in terms of

    a)*   action verbs.
    b)   interpretive verbs.
    c)   state verbs.
    d)   trait descriptions.

Integrative Essay Questions

1. Explain the difference between linguistic relativity and linguistic determinism. What role does cross-cultural research play in the evaluation of each of these hypotheses? Why are within-language

studies important to tests of linguistic determinism?

2. Explain what is meant by codability. How is codability related to tests of the Sapir-Whorf hypothesis? Give some concrete examples of relevant research.

3. What do you feel is the strongest evidence available that supports at least a weak version of linguistic determinism? Why do you think this makes the best case for the existence of linguistic determinism?

4. Give an example of a situation in which the linguistic intergroup bias might apply. How could this bias help maintain stereotypes even in the face of evidence that the stereotype is not accurate?

Chapter 5
The Recognition of Spoken Words

Keeping an Eye on the Big Picture

From the students' point of view, the material in this chapter represents something of a paradox. If a process seems to work effortlessly, as speech recognition does most of the time, what is there to be studied? Where's the problem for science to solve? And yet, it is just such cases where we have an ability that works very rapidly and automatically that the modularity thesis may best apply. Thus, speech recognition is a good place to start if we are to determine, from the standpoint of processing models, the seams between the alleged language modules and more general cognitive abilities.

Therefore, it is important for students to see right away that there are deeply challenging questions to be answered regarding how speech recognition works. In the chapter, I present this in terms of the discrepancy between the ease with which humans process speech versus the great difficulties scientists have had in creating mechanical speech recognition systems. There are other ways to introduce the important issues, of course, and some of these work particularly well in a classroom setting. For example, you can make a tape of someone speaking a foreign language that is unfamiliar to most or all of your students. Have the students try to repeat the sentences, and have them try to transcribe some of the sentences phonetically. Challenge them to pick out where the word boundaries are. Then show them what the sentences were and where the word boundaries are. In this context, you can introduce basic facts about the nature of speech stimuli and then introduce each of the major "problems" that speech recognition poses. Once students have an appreciation for the complexities of the speech recognition process, they can better understand why a special module might be used. I like the analogy of going to the doctor for a diagnosis. If it is something straightforward, your general practitioner may handle it without consulting anyone else. But if he or she sees that it is something more complex, then you are referred to a specialist. This analogy helps students see the plausibility of having the auditory system shunt speech signals to a specialized module for further processing. Students, however, have taught me that it is important to remind them that finding an appealing analogy is not the same as finding evidence.

The Devilish Details

The Nature of the Speech Signal

Most students are relatively unfamiliar with the nature of speech signals and with the technology for synthesizing speech. Fortunately, the availability of speech samples and databases is increasing. In addition, if your students have Internet access, there are several interesting "hands-on"

Copyright © Houghton Mifflin Company. All rights reserved.

experiences available on-line. A good place to start looking for information on speech database sources and software that may be of use to your class is:

www.speech.usyd.edu.au/comp.speech/

A particularly good site for the students to explore is the Haskins Laboratories home page. In the "TOOLS" area of this site there are several easy-to-use demonstrations that allow students to hear samples of synthetic speech and to compare specific samples to the corresponding speech spectrograms. This site can be found at:

www.haskins.yale.edu/haskins/inside.html

Categorical Perception and the Motor Theory

It is easy for students to overlook the fact that at least one common interpretation of the data on categorical perception involves a rather startling claim. An analogy may help. You can present an ordered set of visual stimuli that gradually change from a clear exemplar of one type to a clear exemplar of another type. For example, start with a figure that is clearly a "3" and show several intermediate steps in which the curves on the left side of the figure are successively lengthened until the figure is clearly an "8." The interesting conclusion drawn from categorical perception experiments is that when the speech recognition system analyzes intermediate stimuli, analogous to the intermediate visual stimuli, it doesn't "see" them as intermediate. You can then go on to explain how we wouldn't expect this from a strict auditory processing standpoint, so the motor theory proposes that the categorical effect arises out of the speech processing system, which is separable from the general auditory system. Finally, you can connect this with duplex perception experiments in which, according to motor theory, we are getting a different perceptual experience from the output of each system.

Categorical Perception and the FLMP

The idea that categorical perception makes a strong case for a special speech module has been challenged, of course. You might contrast Massaro's FLMP with the motor theory by working from the previous example I mentioned in which 3s gradually merge into 8s. Ask the students what they would expect if people were shown the various patterns in random order and were asked to classify each one as a "3" or an "8" Of course, people could classify each one, but you would expect the intermediate forms to be classified more slowly than forms closer to the ideal, or prototypical, version of each number. This same typicality phenomenon in speech research has been the foundation of Massaro's critique of the "speech is special" view.

The FLMP is presented in the text as an important example of a challenge to the "speech is special" view, but there are certainly other views of the units of speech recognition and of categorical perception that could be included in lecture. For example, Carol Fowler's view, based on the direct perception tradition, can be used as an interesting contrast to the views discussed in the chapter. For representative samples of her work, see Fowler, Trieman, and Gross (1993) and Dekle, Fowler, and Funnell (1992).

Copyright © Houghton Mifflin Company. All rights reserved.

Chapter 5

Top-Down Processing and Models of Speech Recognition

In the suggestions for helping the students master the material covered in Chapter 3, I noted that it is possible to create a simulation of an interactive model of word recognition with students as nodes in a multilayered network. That demonstration can be adapted easily to the two models discussed in Chapter 5. For each model, you may want to note examples of the interactions among stages that represent bottom-up processing and top-down processing. When students can identify exactly what constitutes top-down processing, they can better understand the differences among the models in terms of how recognition is affected by context. This activity can be repeated at the end of Chapter 6, after more models of word recognition have been discussed.

Multiple Choice Test Items

1. Differences in the frequencies of sound waves are perceived as differences in

    a)   loudness.
    b)*   pitch.
    c)   steady-states.
    d)   Hertz.

2. Differences in the amplitudes of sound waves are perceived as differences in

    a)*   loudness.
    b)   pitch.
    c)   steady-states.
    d)   Hertz.

3. In a speech spectrogram, ___ is shown along the vertical axis and ___ is shown along the horizontal axis.

    a)*   frequency; time
    b)   time; frequency
    c)   frequency; amplitude
    d)   amplitude; frequency

4. In a speech spectrogram, the intensity of the sounds at given frequency is indicated by

    a)   the position on the vertical axis.
    b)   the position on the horizontal axis.
    c)*   how dark a band is shown.
    d)   none of the above.

Copyright © Houghton Mifflin Company. All rights reserved.

5. In a speech spectrogram, the areas that indicate the frequencies at which acoustic energy is concentrated are called

   a) *   formants.
   b)   transitions.
   c)   steady states.
   d)   dynamic segments.

6. In a speech spectrogram, the formant designated F1 is the formant that

   a)   changes most over time.
   b)   remains constant over time.
   c)   is of the greatest intensity.
   d)*   is the one lowest in frequency.

7. One of the reasons that automated speech recognition systems are difficult to develop is that what we consider the same sound, such as the vowel sound in "bat" and "nag", varies a great deal by context. This is known as the _____ problem.

   a)   coarticulation
   b)   speaker variability
   c)*   lack of invariance
   d)   conveyor belt

8. One of the reasons for the lack of invariance problem in speech recognition is that

   a)   speakers do not usually segment their speech.
   b)*   there is coarticulation of phonemes.
   c)   there are few physical differences between similar sounds.
   d)   all of the above

9. Which of the following statements is true?

   a)   Some languages are produced more quickly than others because of differences in coarticulation.
   b)   Pauses do not appear on speech spectrograms.
   c)   The problem of speaker variability refers to individual differences in speaker rates.
   d)*   No two speakers are exactly alike in the production of a particular sound.

Chapter 5

10. In a consonant-vowel-consonant sequence, the information that we need to recognize the vowel sound can be obtained from

    a)   the frequencies of the F1 and F2 steady states.
    b)   the time interval between formant transitions.
    c)   the formant transitions into and out of steady states.
    d)*   all of the above.

11. The time difference between the release of a stop consonant and the vibration of the vocal folds is known as

    a)   the steady state.
    b)   the coarticulation rate.
    c)   phoneme duration time.
    d)*   voice-onset-time.

12. If we vary the voice-onset-time of a syllable in small steps between two easily recognized syllables, people's identification of the intermediate stimuli

    a)   is at chance for the middle position on the voice-onset-time scale.
    b)*   appears to show that all the intermediate stimuli are heard as one of the consonant sounds or the other.
    c)   suggests that they cannot perceive the intermediate sounds.
    d)   is above chance only for the most frequently used syllables in the language.

13. According to the motor theory of speech perception, we don't perceive the differences between various examples of the same syllable because

    a)   we perform a rapid classification of syllables based on prototypes.
    b)   we attend to the invariant part of the signal and ignore irrelevant variation.
    c)*   we encode a sound in terms of the brain's commands for producing that sound.
    d)   all of the above

14. In a duplex perception situation, in which each ear gets one part of a consonant-vowel combination, the person perceives

    a)   the consonant sound in one ear and the vowel sound in the other.
    b)   a nonspeech "chirp" sound.
    c)*   both the speech sound and a nonspeech sound.
    d)   only the speech sound.

Copyright © Houghton Mifflin Company. All rights reserved.

15. When chinchillas were trained to respond differently to two different speech sounds, it was shown that their responses to intermediate speech sounds showed evidence of categorical perception. This finding _____ the motor theory of speech perception.

- a) supports
- b)* undermines
- c) disproves
- d) is irrelevant to

16. In categorical perception experiments, people take longer to say which speech sound a particular stimulus represents when that stimulus is intermediate between two clear examples of speech sounds. This finding

- a)* supports the fuzzy logic model of perception (FLMP).
- b) supports the motor theory of speech perception.
- c) can be used to support either the motor theory or the FLMP.
- d) none of the above

17. According to which of the following theories is speech recognition based on classifying syllables according to the prototypical speech sounds that the syllables are closest to?

- a) the motor theory
- b)* the fuzzy logic model of perception
- c) both a) and b)
- d) none of the above

18. We know that visual and auditory information can become integrated in speech perception because speech perception is altered by hearing one sound produced while seeing another sound produced. This phenomenon is known as

- a)* the McGurk effect.
- b) duplex perception.
- c) coarticulation.
- d) the categorical perception effect.

19. Which of the following theories takes an approach to speech recognition that falls most clearly within the modularity view?

- a)* the motor theory
- b) the fuzzy logic model
- c) the TRACE model
- d) none of the above

Chapter 5

20. Which of the following types of words would you expect to take the *longest* to recognize?

   a) a high frequency word with low frequency neighbors
   b) a high frequency word with high frequency neighbors
   c) a low frequency word with low frequency neighbors
   d)* a low frequency word with high frequency neighbors

21. Which of the following words are in the same phonological neighborhood as the word "king"?

   a) cringe
   b) knight
   c) both a) and b)
   d)* none of the above

22. Which of the following statements is correct regarding recognition of words spoken in a noisy environment?

   a) Recognition is best when a word is spoken in isolation because then there are no segmentation problems.
   b) Recognition will be improved by speaking a word in a sentence context only if the sentence contains a speech error.
   c)* Recognition will be improved by producing a word in a meaningful sentence context.
   d) Recognition is likely to be good because speech and noise are processed by different systems in the brain.

23. Which of the following statements is correct regarding recognition of a word spoken in a noisy environment?

   a) Recognition is poorer if all the words are spoken at the same rate rather than using variations in rate.
   b) Recognition is improved if the speech is synthesized to remove intonations.
   c)* Recognition is better if the words are spoken by a familiar, rather than an unfamiliar, voice.
   d) all of the above.

24. According to the fuzzy logic model, having a supportive context can improve speech recognition by

   a) making the analysis of visual or auditory features more efficient.
   b)* making it easier to integrate the features that have been analyzed.
   c) both a) and b)
   d) none of the above

Copyright © Houghton Mifflin Company. All rights reserved.

25. The phonemic restoration effect

   a) shows that top-down effects in speech override bottom-up processing.
   b)* demonstrates that sentence contexts can create an auditory illusion.
   c) shows that speech is processed by a module that is distinct from other auditory processing.
   d) supports the motor theory of speech perception.

26. Overall, the data on context effects in speech recognition suggest that

   a)* some aspects of word recognition are influenced by context, but context does not necessarily influence the early stages of speech analysis.
   b) sentence contexts more strongly influence acoustic analysis than does the status of the stimulus as a word or nonword.
   c) context effects disprove the hypothesis that "speech is special."
   d) all of the above

27. Which of the following relies most strongly on the idea that recognizing spoken words is based on "the process of elimination?"

   a) the motor theory
   b) the fuzzy logic model
   c)* the cohort model
   d) the TRACE model

28. Which of the following is an example of a connectionist model of word recognition?

   a) the motor theory
   b) the fuzzy logic model
   c) the cohort model
   d)* the TRACE model

29. Which of the following models gives the largest role to the influence of top-down processes in speech recognition?

   a) the motor theory
   b) the fuzzy logic model
   c) the cohort model
   d)* the TRACE model

30. The term *cohort* in the cohort model refers to

    a)   the finding that neighborhood effects are particularly strong in spoken word recognition.
    b)   rhyming words that are activated in the lexicon as the stimulus word is processed.
    c)*   the set of words activated by processing the initial phoneme of a word.
    d)   the last item remaining active after all phonemes of a word have been processed.

31. According to the cohort model, context can affect word recognition by

    a)*   helping to rule out some words that were activated initially.
    b)   speeding up the recognition of the initial phoneme.
    c)   keeping some words that would usually be in the cohort from becoming activated in the first place.
    d)   none of the above

32. Which of the following models of word recognition propose(s) that higher frequency words get more activation from the same speech input than low frequency words?

    a)   the cohort model
    b)   the TRACE model
    c)*   both a) and b)
    d)   none of the above

Integrative Essay Questions

1. Explain why it is easier to get an automated speech recognition system to perform well if it only has to recognize words spoken by a particular individual. Next, imagine that you wanted to improve the performance of an automated system by having it make use of top-down processing in word recognition. What kinds of information would you have to build into the system's memory?

2. Can the cohort model be combined with either the motor theory or the FLMP as a more complete theory of speech recognition? Could the TRACE model be combined with either motor theory or the FLMP? Explain.

3. Explain how synthetic speech signals are created and manipulated in order to determine the perceptual units involved in speech recognition. Does evidence on the role of prosody in speech recognition raise concerns about the use of synthetic speech as a stimulus?

4. The word "dog" is recognized faster than the word "distance" at the end of a sentence beginning with, "The boy walked the…." Contrast the explanations for this effect that would be provided by the cohort model and the TRACE model.

Copyright © Houghton Mifflin Company. All rights reserved.

Chapter 6
Visual Word Recognition

Keeping an Eye on the Big Picture

The jump from spoken to visual word recognition is bigger than many students appreciate. The ability to process spoken language is an evolutionary adaptation; hence it makes sense to consider the extent to which "speech is special." However, because written language is a human invention, it makes no sense to consider whether visual word recognition is handled by a specially dedicated brain circuitry with which we come equipped. So the major question for this chapter shifts to the issue of whether we learn to recognize written words by grafting visual analysis onto the preexisting speech recognition system.

It is helpful to note that this is not just a question of theoretical interest. Many of the ongoing debates about reading instruction in general, and about reading disabilities in particular, center on the role of speech sounds in visual word recognition. I find that many students in my classes have heard of the debate among reading educators over the "phonics" versus the "whole language" approach. Moreover, a sizable percentage of the students have an interest in dyslexia because they have friends or relatives labeled as dyslexic or because they have been so labeled themselves. Therefore, it is not difficult to relate the broad theoretical question that guides this chapter back to applied questions that are of interest to the students. Unfortunately, the familiarity of these issues also has a down side: students often come into the class with some well-entrenched misconceptions. It is unlikely that these misconceptions can be overcome simply by reading accurate information in a text. It will probably take activities and classroom discussion to effectively counter the most prevalent of the misconceptions about dyslexia and reading acquisition. I have found it helpful to have students bring in articles or product advertisements that make claims about helping those with reading problems. The information in this chapter can be used as background critical evaluations of these articles or ads. In addition, the Internet offers ample opportunity to find both wheat and chaff with regard to information on dyslexia. I find that when students have really mastered the material in this chapter they can separate wheat from chaff and explain their basis for doing so. If you do an Internet project of this kind, and you want to show the students a good example of a balanced presentation on the issue of dyslexia, one of the better sites can be found at:

www.greenwood.org/resta.html

which is sponsored by the Greenwood Institute.

The Devilish Details

Orthography and the Dual-Route Model

A good way to introduce students to the notion of different routes to word recognition is to teach them a new word. The first time students see the word *contumelious*, which means contemptuous, they will probably try to slowly sound-out the word. However, if you show them the word several times over a series of classes, they will certainly get the feeling that they can quickly recognize the word without going through the sounding out process. The students could still be accessing a phonological code even after extensive exposure, but they are no longer relying on subvocal articulation. You can use this activity as a bridge to discussing what is meant by the assembled route and how the idea of accessing a phonological code is different from laboriously sounding out a word.

There are a number of activities that can be carried out in the classroom to strengthen students' appreciation for the relationship between orthographic depth and the ease of using an assembled route for word recognition. One such activity is to present students with novel words created by making irregularly spelled words more regular. For example, you can remove the silent letters from words like *debt, subtle,* and *castle*. Ask the students how such a change would affect the ease of using an assembled route. Should we have spelling reform to make words both easier to spell and easier to learn to read? Would we lose anything in such a step? What about removing the silent letter from a word like *sign*? Clearly, we'd have to use some kind of marking to indicate the long vowel sound, but we'd still lose the morphological level of regularity that shows the relation between *sign* and *signify*.

The Word Superiority Effect Versus Sublexical Processing

If you have access to a computer or some decent film equipment, it is not difficult to create a word superiority effect demonstration. The effect is quite obvious, even after only a few trials. However, this compelling effect can also cause students to become confused about an apparent paradox. If the word superiority effect means that we recognize words as wholes, rather than letter-by-letter, how can there also be sublexical processing units? The mental trap here is, of course, the erroneous implication that the word superiority effect means that we always process words in terms of a single wholistic entity. It is often helpful to work carefully through how the word superiority effect implies parallel processing of letters but not that there are no sublexical units that are functional in recognition. Of course, as the text describes, there is continuing disagreement over exactly what units are functional in recognition. Despite the complexities of the studies in this area, it is not difficult to demonstrate the general notion of the importance of sublexical units. You can time the students as they read brief passages of varying lengths and then run correlations between reading time and three different measures of passage length: number of letters, number of syllables, and number of words. In most cases, number of syllables will be the best predictor of reading time.

Copyright © Houghton Mifflin Company. All rights reserved.

Chapter 6

Multiple Choice Test Items

1. A writing system that uses a unique symbol for each word or morpheme is known as a ___ system.

    a)* logographic
    b) syllabic
    c) alphabetic
    d) tonal

2. A language in which the change in pitch of a vowel can signify a morphemic distinction is known as a ___ language.

    a) logographic
    b) syllabic
    c) alphabetic
    d)* tonal

3. The writing system in Chinese is an example of a logographic system. This means that Chinese

    a) uses a stylized picture to symbolize each word.
    b) uses arbitrary symbols to represent syllables.
    c) uses arbitrary symbols to represent sounds.
    d)* uses arbitrary symbols to represent morphemes.

4. If you are told that a particular language has a "deep orthography," then you know that the language uses a(n) ____ system of writing.

    a) logographic
    b) syllabic
    c)* alphabetic
    d) any of the above are possible

5. Given that the Japanese *kana* writing system is syllabic, you can infer that the number of allowable syllable combinations in Japanese is

    a) about the same as in English.
    b) many more than in English.
    c)* many fewer than in English.
    d) none of the above.

Copyright © Houghton Mifflin Company. All rights reserved.

6. A writing system in which a different letter of the alphabet is used for each phoneme in the language would be a language that

        a)   is more efficient than any known language.
        b)   would best capture tonal qualities.
        c)   would have the deepest orthography.
        d)*   would have the shallowest orthography.

7. A major reason that English has a fairly deep orthography is that

        a)   it optimally represents morphemic relationships among words.
        b)*   it has many words that are borrowed from other languages.
        c)   spelling has become more simplified over time to increase spelling-to-sound correspondence.
        d)   all of the above

8. A major problem with the template approach to word recognition is that

        a)   templates could only be used with alphabetic writing systems.
        b)   templates could only be used with syllabic writing systems.
        c)   people could not store templates in memory.
        d)*   our word recognition ability handles variations too well to be explained by templates.

9. The *Pandemonium* model explains

        a)   word recognition in terms of feature analysis on whole words.
        b)   the word superiority effect.
        c)   how top-down sources of activation influence letter recognition.
        d)*   none of the above.

10. The *Pandemonium* model explains

        a)*   how features might be used to recognize letters.
        b)   why words are easier to recognize than single letters.
        c)   how the context a letter appears in influences recognition of that letter.
        d)   the processing difficulties experienced by dyslexic readers.

11. Compared to the *Pandemonium* model, the interactive activation view relies more on the idea that

        a)   several letters are processed in parallel during word recognition.
        b)   there are both top-down and bottom-up processes in word recognition.
        c)   there is inhibition as well as activation during processing.
        d)*   all of the above

12. If one of the following was flashed very briefly on a screen, which one would give you the best chance of accurately saying that the letter "C" had been presented?

   a)   C
   b)   ACIG
   c)* LACE
   d)   XCX

13. The interactive activation model explains the word superiority effect in terms of

   a)* top-down influences from the word level to earlier levels of analysis.
   b)   inhibition of infrequent words.
   c)   top-down influences from the feature level to the word level.
   d)   higher baseline activation levels of high-frequency words.

14. We could recognize words by associating letters or syllables with their corresponding speech sounds. This is known as the ___ route to word recognition.

   a)   interactive activation
   b)* assembled
   c)   direct
   d)   dual

15. We could recognize words by associating visual word forms with entries in the lexicon. This is known as the ___ route to word recognition.

   a)   interactive activation
   b)   assembled
   c)* direct
   d)   dual

16. People are most likely to use an assembled route to word recognition in a language that has a writing system with

   a)* a shallow orthography, for example, Serbo-Croatian .
   b)   a deep orthography, for example, Hebrew.
   c)   an orthography of intermediate depth, for example, English.
   d)   none of the above.

17. In English, which has a writing system of intermediate orthographic depth, words are recognized via

        a)   the direct route.
        b)   the assembled route.
        c)*   both the direct and the assembled routes.
        d)   the direct route for normal readers and the assembled route for dyslexic readers.

18. Which of the following is evidence that we chunk words at morphemic boundaries during word recognition?

        a)   Some words, like *repertoire*, only seem to have a prefix.
        b)*   Words with prefixes or suffixes prime their root words.
        c)   Familiar groups of letters in long words prime other words with the same groups of letters.
        d)   all of the above

19. Which of the following words is most likely to be recognized using the direct route?

        a)   fey
        b)   calamity
        c)*   love
        d)   harden

20. Regularity of spelling-to-sound correspondence predicts word recognition times for

        a)   high-frequency words.
        b)*   low-frequency words.
        c)   words at all frequency levels.
        d)   none of the above.

21. If word recognition were based on searching through groups of words in the lexicon in a serial fashion, then we would expect that the recognition times would ____ neighborhood size.

        a)*   increase with increases in
        b)   decrease with increases in
        c)   be unaffected by

22. There is evidence that the effect of a large neighborhood on visual word recognition

        a)   depends on word frequency.
        b)   can be facilitative.
        c)   can be inhibitory.
        d)*   all of the above

Chapter 6

23. When reading a text, people typically

    a) control their reading rate by changing the number of fixations they make.
    b) make longer saccades when the text is difficult.
    c) make longer saccades when the text is easy.
    d)* fixate almost every word.

24. If you monitor eye fixations in reading passages, you find that the typical reader fixates

    a) for about 300 milliseconds on almost every word.
    b) for about 300 milliseconds on each major content word.
    c)* on almost every word, but the duration of each fixation varies greatly.
    d) on only the major content words, but the duration of each fixation varies greatly.

25. Studies that have used sentence or paragraph contexts as primes for single words have shown that

    a)* context effects are often small, but there is evidence for top-down influences.
    b) visual word recognition is a bottom-up process.
    c) the longer the context, the stronger the top-down influence on visual word recognition.
    d) if the context is semantically related to the target word, top-down processes are predominant.

26. The term *logogen* refers to

    a) an entry in the lexicon.
    b) a pattern recognizer that monitors orthographic information.
    c) a pattern recognizer that monitors semantic information.
    d)* all of the above.

27. The logogen model of word recognition accounts for frequency effects in terms of the

    a) size of the neighborhood that is activated for high-frequency versus low-frequency words.
    b) top-down connections from the word level to the letter level.
    c) order in which words are searched in the lexicon.
    d)* different resting levels of activation of the entries in the lexicon.

28. In the logogen model of word recognition,

    a) the lexicon is organized in a list format.
    b) large neighborhood size can facilitate, but never inhibit, word recognition.
    c)* sentence context can increase the activation of a specific logogen.
    d) all of the above

Copyright © Houghton Mifflin Company. All rights reserved.

29. In the autonomous search model,

   a)* the lexicon is searched in order of frequency.
   b) sentence contexts eliminate the need to search the lexicon.
   c) large neighborhoods are searched more slowly than small neighborhoods.
   d) all of the above

30. The term *autonomous* in the autonomous search model refers to the idea that

   a) only one lexical entry can be activated at any given time.
   b)* contexts do not influence the process of initial lexical access for a particular word.
   c) the lexicon is divided into independent parts, the access files and the master lexicon.
   d) each access file is searched independently without influencing the searches of other access files.

31. Compared to the other models of word recognition you studied, the connectionist model

   a) relies more on the idea of inhibitory connections among some parts of the lexical network.
   b) gives a more prominent role to top-down processes.
   c) more clearly predicts the existence of neighborhood effects.
   d)* all of the above

32. The data that suggest that syllables serve as basic units of word recognition are most challenging to the

   a) logogen model.
   b) autonomous search model.
   c)* connectionist model.
   d) none of the above

33. Which of the following claims is most widely accepted by the scientists who study visual word recognition?

   a) Context can affect lexical decisions but not lexical access.
   b) Context can affect the bottom-up flow of information.
   c)* Multiple word candidates are activated and compete for selection.
   d) Lexical entries are best represented in a distributed fashion.

34. Any child who is having difficulty relative to his or her peers in learning to read

   a) is considered to be dyslexic.
   b) has specific reading disability but may or may not have dyslexia.
   c) is considered dyslexic unless specific brain damage has been identified.
   d)* none of the above

35. People with dyslexia most often have problems with

   a)*   the phonological route to word recognition.
   b)   reversing letters.
   c)   processing visual features.
   d)   all of the above.

36. In comparing good and poor readers on their use of context to identify words, Stanovich has found that

   a)   both groups use context about equally.
   b)   good readers use context, but poor readers usually do not.
   c)   neither good readers nor poor readers make much use of context to identify words.
   d)*   poor readers tend to use context more than good readers.

37. Interactive compensatory processing refers to

   a)   the tendency of normal readers to use context to help them understand new words.
   b)*   the tendency for poor readers to use context to guess at words they cannot encode easily.
   c)   the ability to use activation at the word level to augment the visual analysis of words.
   d)   a program that has shown some success in treating dyslexia.

Integrative Essay Questions

1. Is it possible to formulate an interactive-search model of visual word recognition? How would such a model explain frequency effects and context effects?

2. Let's say that you believe that when people read in unfamiliar fonts, **such as the font shown here**, they make more use of the assembled route to word recognition. How could this hypothesis be tested?

3. How might the orthographic depth of a writing system be related to the issue of the sublexical units involved in word recognition? For example, would preserving morphological relations in the orthography at the expense of some spelling-to-sound regularity influence which sublexical units are functional? How could you test this empirically?

4. Your neighbor has a third-grade child who has had a great deal of difficulty learning to read. Your neighbor sees an infomercial that advertises special glasses, which the advertiser claims gives correction for the visual processing problems of most dyslexics. What would you tell your neighbor? What evidence would you use to support your position?

Copyright © Houghton Mifflin Company. All rights reserved.

Chapter 7
Sentence Processing

Keeping an Eye on the Big Picture

By now the students have been given considerable background on the issue of modular versus interactive approaches to cognition in general and language in particular. The principal aim of this chapter is to now tackle the question of modularity head-on because much of the research on sentence processing has focused on this very issue. To be sure that the students are prepared to take on this subject, you may want to open this section of your course with a comparison of the two approaches.

I have found that students benefit from considering what advantages there might be to each type of system. The students typically have an easier time seeing that an interactive system might be better because you are taking more information into account as a stimulus is processed. However, a case can be made that such a system could lead to confusions and delays in sorting out conflicting information. With some encouragement, students can come to appreciate the strengths and weaknesses of both approaches.

In discussing the strengths and weaknesses of each approach, it is useful to compare and contrast the general kinds of evidence that proponents of each type of theory tend to cite. Interactive theorists tend to point out the plausibility of the approach at a neural level, while modular theorists tend to focus on the study of the syndromes that result from brain damage. More recently, there has been an increase in noting the evolutionary plausibility of some modular approaches (e.g., Pinker, 1997). It is worth noting the danger of running way ahead of any empirical evidence in these discussions of evolutionary plausibility. The dangers of such post hoc "just so" stories are well documented (e.g., Dupré, 1987). In fact, this is related to a general criticism often made of *both* approaches: they may be too powerful to adequately constrain theory generation and testing.

Depending on how sophisticated your students are about computational modeling, you could introduce a discussion here that covers the criticisms of connectionist models, though it is important to point out that an interactive approach is not necessarily connectionist and that it is possible to have connectionist layers within an overall modular system.

The Devilish Details

Lexical Access and Context

Studies of how people resolve lexical ambiguities in context have been at the forefront of the battle over modularity for some time, so I focused on these studies in the chapter. However, it is also important for students to think about this material as very related to the other context effects we examined in the previous two chapters. You may want to contrast one of the studies from previous chapters that looked at context effects on lexical decision or naming with similar study of resolution of lexical ambiguity (e.g., Onifer & Swinney, 1981). Have the students consider how tracing the time course of meaning activation from an ambiguous target word is especially important to the modularity hypothesis. It may also be useful to compare the time course of activation for meanings of ambiguous words with the data from Neely's (1977) classic study, which was mentioned in Chapter 3. The students should be able to see how the time course of activation in the ambiguity studies is consistent with the interpretation that whether lexical access is context-dependent or context-independent, it is occurring automatically.

Syntactic Ambiguity and Parsing

Students generally have some difficulty understanding the two syntactic parsing strategies that are discussed in the chapter, late closure and minimal attachment. In addition, students may need some active exercises in order to appreciate how purely syntactic parsing strategies are different from the "evidence-based view" discussed in the chapter. One useful exercise to clarify these concepts is to have the students generate their own garden-path sentences that are based on violating default parsing strategies. Then, you can add semantic cues to the correct resolution and discuss whether the semantic context might reduce the garden-path effect. Here's an example (based on late closure) that you can use to get the students started:

After William settles a dispute always breaks out among his coworkers.

Compare that sentence with the next two, which provide different directions of contextual bias:

After William, a lawyer, settles a dispute always breaks out among his coworkers.

After William gets into his chair and settles a dispute always breaks out among his coworkers.

Metaphoric Sentences

As with the issue of context effects on lexical access, this chapter's discussion of metaphor represents the culmination of an issue developed in several earlier portions of the text. In particular, it is well worth reminding students of Lakoff's work on semantics, which was presented in Chapter 2. A major contention of his view is that metaphor is not ornamental: it is woven into the very fabric of language. That same general idea is central to the single-stage view discussed in Chapter 7. A useful way to explore this idea further is through the conceptual metaphor home page found at the following address:

http://cogsci.berkeley.edu/

Using this page, students can trace the relationships among many different metaphoric expressions found in the English language.

Copyright © Houghton Mifflin Company. All rights reserved.

Chapter 7

Another useful site for reinforcing the concepts discussed in Chapter 7 is the home page of the Center for the Cognitive Science of Metaphor, which can be found at:

http://metaphor.uoregon.edu/metaphor.html

A number of brief papers are available there. Many of them are written at a level that undergraduate students will find understandable.

Multiple Choice Test Items

1. If you obtained data that suggested that people use syntactic parsing strategies and semantic information at the same time in order to determine the syntactic roles of words and clauses in a sentence, then the data would support

    a)   the modular view.
    b)*   the interactive view.
    c)   a combination of the modular and the interactive views.
    d)   the late closure hypothesis.

2. Fillenbaum (1974) found that people, without even realizing it, may include "corrections" when they paraphrase anomalous sentences like, "John dressed and had a bath." These data demonstrate that

    a)   syntactic parsing occurs before semantic analysis.
    b)   syntactic and pragmatic information is used jointly in comprehension.
    c)   syntactic manipulations are irrelevant to sentence memory.
    d)*   none of the above

3. The term "immediacy of interpretation" refers to the idea that during sentence processing

    a)   lexical access is performed before other processes such as syntactic analysis can begin.
    b)   we use context to access the appropriate meaning of an ambiguous word.
    c)   we initially access both appropriate and inappropriate meanings of an ambiguous word.
    d)*   we try to understand each word and integrate into the context as soon as possible.

4. Which of the following is an example of a garden-path sentence?

    a)   The professor warned the students that passing his course was difficult.
    b)   The bug that was on the floor was never seen.
    c)*   The reporter told about the corruption was interested.
    d)   none of the above.

Copyright © Houghton Mifflin Company. All rights reserved.

5. Which of the following sentences is ungrammatical?

   a) The professor warned the students that passing his course was difficult.
   b) The bug that was on the floor was never seen.
   c) The reporter told about the corruption was interested.
   d)* none of the above.

6. Which of the following statements is true?

   a) Polysemy, though infrequent, is useful for controlled experiments that test whether lexical access is modular.
   b) Polysemous words are exceptions to the principle of immediacy of interpretation.
   c)* Polysemy is common in samples of natural language.
   d) none of the above

7. Whether an investigator finds evidence for multiple or selective access of ambiguous word meanings depends, at least in part, on

   a) whether a dominant or subordinate meaning is intended.
   b) how strongly biasing the context is.
   c) whether the biasing context occurs before or after the ambiguous word.
   d)* all of the above.

8. When you test the modularity of lexical access by examining the processing of ambiguous words in context, the modularity hypothesis is strongly supported if

   a)* multiple meanings are activated even in contexts that clearly suggest a particular meaning.
   b) dominant meanings are activated when the context is weak.
   c) meaning selection takes place very quickly.
   d) all of the above

9. In the study by Duffy and associates (1988), which was discussed in the text, reading times for ambiguous words were longer than reading times for unambiguous control words when

   a) the reader had to maintain two different meanings of an ambiguous word.
   b) the context had not yet biased a particular meaning of an equibiased homograph.
   c) a subordinate meaning was biased by the context early in the sentence.
   d)* all of the above

10. With regard to syntactic parsing, the modularity view predicts that

- a) syntactic parsing follows semantic analysis of the sentence.
- b) initial syntactic parsing depends on a combination of syntax-based strategies and semantic analysis.
- c) syntactic parsing is part of lexical access.
- d)* initial syntactic parsing is unaffected by semantic context.

11. In syntactic parsing, the strategy of attaching a new clause to the most recently processed clause is known as

- a) modular parsing.
- b) interactive parsing.
- c)* late closure.
- d) minimal attachment.

12. In syntactic parsing, the strategy of attaching new clauses in a way that results in the fewest nodes in the phrase structure tree is known as

- a) modular parsing.
- b) interactive parsing.
- c) late closure.
- d)* minimal attachment.

13. Consider the sentence, "The biologist examined the tissue culture with a microscope." The idea that the biologist is using the microscope is favored by

- a)* both semantics and minimal attachment.
- b) semantics but not minimal attachment.
- c) both minimal attachment and late closure.
- d) late closure, but not semantics.

14. According to Frazier (1987), we use minimal attachment and late closure strategies in parsing as a way of

- a) allowing semantics and syntax to interact as early as possible.
- b) resolving lexical ambiguities.
- c)* minimizing the cognitive load of syntactic parsing.
- d) none of the above

15. The "evidence-based" approach to syntactic ambiguity holds that

   a)   multiple possible syntactic structures for a sentence may be activated.
   b)   both syntactic and semantic information may be used to parse a sentence.
   c)   how frequently a particular syntactic structure is used affects parsing.
   d)* all of the above.

16. The "evidence-based" approach to syntactic parsing differs from the modular view espoused by Frazier and associates in that

   a)   the modular view argues that semantics is never involved in parsing.
   b)* the evidence-based view is an example of an interactive view of parsing.
   c)   the evidence-based view can account for the rapid time course of parsing in most sentences.
   d)   all of the above

17. In a series of experiments, Tanenhaus and colleagues monitored eye movements as people examined a visual display and heard sentences like, "Put the saltshaker on the envelope in the bowl." These experiments showed that

   a)   regardless of the visual context, the sentence is initially parsed so that "envelope" refers to the location of the saltshaker.
   b)* visual context may override the tendency to use minimal attachment to parse the sentence.
   c)   regardless of the visual context, the sentence is initially parsed so that "envelope" refers to the place where the saltshaker should be moved.
   d)   visual context cannot override minimal attachment, but may speed parsing when it matches the default assumptions.

18. Research on the parsing of spoken sentences suggests that

   a)   immediacy of interpretation is our general operating principle
   b)   the information in visual displays can influence initial syntactic parsing
   c)   prosodic cues can assist us in sentence parsing.
   d)* all of the above

19. Which of the following statements represents a point of agreement between modular and interactive theories of parsing?

   a)   The initial parsing of a sentence is based on purely syntactic principles.
   b)   "Syntax proposes and semantics disposes."
   c)* The final parsing of any particular sentence may be based on syntactic, semantic, and prosodic information.
   d)   all of the above.

Chapter 7

20. Which of the following terms is closest in meaning to "compositional semantics"?

  a)* locutionary meaning
  b) illocutionary force
  c) speech act
  d) metaphor

21. Which of the following terms is closest in meaning to illocutionary force?

  a) metaphor
  b)* speech act
  c) indirect speech act
  d) magna carta

22. Which of the following sentences is an indirect speech act?

  a) Love is a red red rose.
  b) My surgeon was a butcher.
  c)* Do you have the time?
  d) all of the above

23. Which of the following is an example of figurative language?

  a) Could you please open a window?
  b) Time is money.
  c) Your smile outshines the brightest stars.
  d)* all of the above

24. Which of the following sentences is a speech act?

  a)* We find the defendant not guilty.
  b) Please leave.
  c) Could you just go?
  d) all of the above

25. The idea that we first try to come up with a literal interpretation of a sentence before evaluating it for figurative content is central to the

  a) single-stage view.
  b)* three-stage view.
  c) conceptual-metaphor theory.
  d) none of the above

Copyright © Houghton Mifflin Company. All rights reserved.

26. According to Grice, we can make sense of conversations because people generally follow certain guidelines. For example, the maxim of quantity says that speakers should

 a) say everything they know to be true.
 b) avoid ambiguity.
 c) relate new utterances to previous ones.
 d)* say as much as is necessary to be informative.

27. According to Grice, we can make sense of conversations because people generally follow certain guidelines. For example, the maxim of manner says that speakers should

 a) say everything they know to be true.
 b)* avoid ambiguity.
 c) relate new utterances to previous ones.
 d) say as much as is necessary to be informative.

28. According to the ___ view of figurative comprehension, speakers sometimes violate Grice's maxims as a cue that nonliteral interpretation is intended.

 a) the single-stage
 b)* the three-stage
 c) class-inclusion
 d) schema

29. In the metaphoric statement, "Time is money," *time* is the topic and *money* is the

 a) ground.
 b) quality.
 c) emergent feature.
 d)* vehicle.

30. Compared to their literal counterparts, figurative statements tend to

 a) take longer to comprehend.
 b) be less memorable.
 c)* communicate feelings more effectively.
 d) all of the above

Chapter 7

31. An argument against the three-stage view of figurative language comprehension and in support of the single-stage view is that

    a)   some sentences are not easy to classify as either literal or figurative.
    b)   figurative interpretations often take no more time than literal ones.
    c)   there is considerable overlap in the processes used to comprehend literal and figurative statements.
    d)*   all of the above

32. If we understand a metaphor as a class inclusion statement, then clearly this classification involves emergent features. Emergent features

    a)*   are part of the ground, but not the topic or the vehicle.
    b)   involve the transfer of a feature from the topic to the vehicle.
    c)   involve the transfer of a feature from the topic to the ground.
    d)   involve the transfer of a feature from the vehicle to the topic.

Integrative Essay Questions

1. Define the principle of immediacy of interpretation. How does this principle relate to the debate between modular and interactive views of syntactic parsing? Does immediacy of interpretation also hold when the ongoing interpretation is figurative? Justify your answer with evidence.

2. Describe the strongest evidence in favor of the idea that lexical access is autonomous. What evidence provides the strongest support for the autonomy of syntactic parsing? Can the data you have discussed be handled by interactive approaches to lexical and syntactic processing?

3. Discuss how figurative processing permeates language at the lexical, sentence, and passage levels.

4. Draw a diagram that represents the general stages of processing the sentence, "My teacher is a lighthouse to students." How does the information flow among the stages differ for modular and interactive views?

Copyright © Houghton Mifflin Company. All rights reserved.

Chapter 8
Understanding and Remembering Discourse

Keeping an Eye on the Big Picture

The focus of this chapter is on how the many different types of language-specific and general cognitive mechanisms that were studied in the previous chapters are organized and applied as we comprehend discourse. A useful class demonstration for getting the students prepared for an inquiry into discourse processing is to have them read a text of 100 words or so. Then have half the class summarize the text and have the other half try to recall the text as closely as possible to the original wording. After discussing what information did, and did not, make it into the summaries and the longer recall attempts, you can sketch a model of the memory system with working memory, semantic memory, and episodic memory all indicated. Have the students discuss how the text was comprehended and recalled in terms of the ways that different parts of the memory system were employed. Have them consider how the use of the memory system differs for summarization versus full recall. It is also helpful to save at least some of the representative summarization and recall protocols to illustrate some of the phenomena that come up in the chapter or in your lectures.

Another useful class activity is to finish off this material by considering the implications of what the students have learned for how information should be presented in multimedia environments. Many interesting questions can be raised: Are more hypertext key words and more options for moving through the material always going to be better? Does it matter whether you want the person using the system to develop a textbase representation or a mental model? Can the same setup be optimized for both good and poor comprehenders? Some thought-provoking discussions of these kinds of issues can be found at the Human Communication Research Centre's website:

www.hcrc.ed.ac.uk

This site also has information and project descriptions on a number of other topics that are relevant to discourse processing, including resolution of anaphora and discourse coherence.

The Devilish Details

Minimalist and Constructivist Views of Text Processing

It is easy for students (and even some professionals in the field!) to lapse into dichotomous thinking whereby they feel they must decide whether people make inferences promiscuously during comprehension or they make almost no inferences beyond those directly required for local coherence. It is important to avoid this misconception without ignoring the fact that fairly extreme positions on the minimalist-constructivist continuum have been, and continue to be, espoused.

One way to make it clear that there are different possible positions along the continuum and to show why the general issue is important is to relate how the views on elaboration during comprehension are important in some applied areas that the students can appreciate. For example, if you are on a jury, then comprehending and remembering discourse becomes a critical, even life and death, matter. The processing of testimony is a straightforward context in which to stake out the differences between constructivist and minimalist views. The jury situation is also a context, outside of the narrative reading context of most experiments in this area, in which to demonstrate that cause-effect linkages among propositions may be the central organizing principle of the memory representations.

The Concept of Multiple Text Representations

The idea that we form not one but two or three mental representations of a passage has become a key notion in psycholinguistics. Unfortunately, this key idea is likely to remain quite fuzzy in the minds of the students unless they get some practice at differentiating among the different types of representations. One common misconception is to think of a macrostructure, which is what people use when they generate a summary (as in the introductory exercise I suggested), as the same thing as a mental model. Another common misconception to watch out for is the idea that the mental model has to be a visual image. If you started this section of the course with a recall demonstration, you can have the students examine the protocols and identify what elements in the recall do not come strictly from the text itself, and thus originate in a mental model, and which come from a textbase representation. You may want to point out that the textbase and the mental model can simultaneously serve as sources of information for recall. Thus, it can be difficult to separate the two representations through analysis of recall. That is why the key experiments differentiating the content of the two representations that are mentioned in the text are based on recognition data.

Another way to help clarify the difference between the textbase and model representations is to integrate these concepts with the information on differences between narrative and expository genres. Clearly, the textbase follows the same organization pattern as the text itself, but the model representation may be organized on a completely different basis. To make this clear you may want to have the students analyze a narrative text and an expository text using the schemes presented on pages 249 and 253. To give them the general idea of the expository genre, you could have the students classify the different levels of the outline of one of the chapters in their text for this class. You might also want the students to do the same analysis on a set of instructions and then have the

Copyright © Houghton Mifflin Company. All rights reserved.

students consider the difference between remembering those instructions as written versus using that information to show someone else how to perform the task. Using information from the chapter, they should be able to talk about reasons why instruction manuals are often hard to understand.

Poor Comprehension Versus Dyslexia

Another misconception that often affects students as they study discourse processing is the idea that dyslexia and poor comprehension ability are the same thing. Chapter 6 of the text presents information on the nature of dyslexia, but the students may not realize that people can have relatively poor comprehension despite being in the normal range at recognizing words. The information on individual differences in comprehension affords a nice opportunity to review all the material in this chapter by having the students propose all the ways that comprehension could, in principle, break down *beyond the stage of lexical access.* Then, you can discuss whether each of these problems is actually found among poor readers and whether some of the possible problems are connected to a single cause.

Multiple Choice Test Items

1. Coherence of a text is established by

   a) linking adjacent sentences together.
   b) relating individual sentences to the main idea of the passage.
   c) relating information in a text to background knowledge.
   d)* all of the above.

2. According to the constructivist view of comprehension

   a) we cannot understand a passage completely unless a meaningful title is provided.
   b)* much of the information used in comprehending a passage comes from our background knowledge.
   c) establishing global coherence is more important than establishing local coherence.
   d) all of the above

3. According to the minimalist view of comprehension,

   a) background information is not used in text comprehension.
   b) the way we read depends on how we expect our memory for the text to be tested.
   c)* our inferences typically are directed toward maintaining local coherence.
   d) we only make those inferences that are required for global coherence.

Copyright © Houghton Mifflin Company. All rights reserved.

4. The view that readers make all possible inferences in order to form a concrete model of a text is a central idea in the _____ view.

      a)   construction-integration
      b)   minimalist
      c)   constructivist
      d)*   none of the above

5. Consider the following pair of sentences:
    Bill was taking his last test in college. *He* was giving it his best shot.
The terms in italics represent which cohesion device?

      a)   lexical
      b)   substitution
      c)*   coreference
      d)   none of the above

6. Consider the following pair of sentences:
    Bill was taking his last test in college. *Bill* was giving it his best shot.
The terms in italics represent which cohesion device?

      a)   ellipsis
      b)   coreference
      c)   conjunction
      d)*   none of the above

7. A cohesion device that is used frequently to indicate a causal connection between two propositions is
      a)   substitution.
      b)   ellipsis.
      c)*   conjunction.
      d)   none of the above

8. In the following sentence: "Gina went to the dance alone, but she ended up having a great time," *Gina* is a(n) ___ and *she* is a(n) ____.

      a)   lexical device; coreferent
      b)   coreferent; lexical device
      c)*   antecedent; anaphor
      d)   anaphor; antecedent

Chapter 8

The next three questions are concerned with an analysis of the following passage:

> John and Marie were taking an extended vacation on Maui. Unfortunately, the luggage went to a different island. Their hotel was gracious enough to loan them some provisions.

9. The use of the definite article, *the*, signals that *luggage* is considered to be ____ in the second sentence.

   a)*   given information
   b)   new information
   c)   a lexical cohesion device
   d)   coreferential

10. Maintaining coherence across the first two sentences requires

    a)*   a bridging inference.
    b)   an elaborative inference.
    c)   overcoming a violation of the given/new contract.
    d)   a mental model.

11. The first word of the third sentence, *their,* is an example of a

    a)   bridging inference.
    b)*   pronominal reference.
    c)   signal that new information will be supplied.
    d)   all of the above

12. The time needed to understand an anaphoric reference has been shown to depend on

    a)   the number of sentences intervening between the antecedent and the anaphor.
    b)   the prominence of the antecedent in a mental model of the passage.
    c)   whether the antecedent was the first noun phrase in a passage.
    d)*   all of the above.

13. The evidence on readers' use of elaborative inferences supports the view that

    a)   readers tend to make instrumental inferences.
    b)   few elaborations are made unless local coherence fails.
    c)*   readers make inferences relevant to the causal explanations for events.
    d)   most readers use context to predict what will happen next in a passage.

Copyright © Houghton Mifflin Company. All rights reserved.

14. A pair of sentences is likely to remembered best if the causal connection between the two sentences is
    a)   very strong and obvious.
    b)*   moderately strong but inferred by the reader.
    c)   very slight so that the reader makes an effortful search for the connection.

15. Global coherence requires that

    a)   each sentence after the first makes a reference to the preceding sentence.
    b)   a title is given that provides the overall context.
    c)   both a) and b)
    d)*   none of the above

16. In comprehension of, and memory for, narrative text the "levels effect" refers to the finding that statements that are higher in the goal hierarchy are ___ than statements lower in the hierarchy.

    a)   read more quickly and are remembered better
    b)   read more slowly and are remembered more poorly
    c)*   read more slowly and are remembered better
    d)   read more quickly and are remembered more poorly

17. Narrative comprehension seems to be based on forming

    a)   associations among descriptions of scenes.
    b)   a mental image of how a scene would appear.
    c)   elaborative inferences.
    d)*   causal connections among the elements of the story.

18. Consider the following brief narrative:
    Jason wanted to go out with Ellen. However, he was afraid of rejection so he decided to ask his friend Tina to find out what Ellen thought of him.
The decision to talk to Tina is an example of

    a)   a superordinate goal.
    b)*   a subordinate goal.
    c)   a setting.
    d)   none of the above

19. One of the major differences between narrative and expository text is that the structure of narrative text

    a)   can have one kind of unit embedded in another.
    b)   joins some units based on cause-effect relations.
    c)*   is less variable than the structure of expository text.
    d)   all of the above

Chapter 8

20. An expository text that is organized around posing a problem and offering a solution is said to have a ____ structure.

    a) collection
    b) causation
    c)* response
    d) description

21. The term "macroprocessing" refers to the process of

    a) skimming a passage to get the main ideas only.
    b) processing a passage very thoroughly so that all elements are well understood.
    c)* keeping track of the theme of a passage and how the details are related to the theme.
    d) establishing local coherence so that all sentences are connected as part of a chain of associations.

22. The reading time for the ___ sentences of an expository passage tend to be relatively long because _____.

    a) last few; more information is being held in working memory.
    b)* first few; the theme of the passage must be well represented in memory.
    c) middle; of the serial position effect.

23. Advance organizers, such as outlines and previews, often improve comprehension by

    a) decreasing the attention allocated to microprocessing.
    b) converting the text to a descriptive structure, which is the simplest structure.
    c)* making macroprocessing easier.
    d) all of the above.

24. The evidence that readers generally form connections between actions and superordinate goals and between thematic statements and details presents difficulty for the

    a)* minimalist view.
    b) constructivist view.
    c) construction-integration theory.
    d) all of the above

25. A key idea of the construction-integration model of discourse processing is the idea that

    a) there are processing cycles.
    b) a bottom-up phase of activation is followed by a phase in which irrelevant activations are pruned.
    c) multiple representations are formed while reading a text.
    d)* all of the above

Copyright © Houghton Mifflin Company. All rights reserved.

26. If elaborative inferences are made during reading, they are included as part of the

   a) surface form.
   b) textbase.
   c)* situational model.
   d) all of the above

27. The paraphrase of a passage is most like which type of mental representation?

   a) the surface form
   b)* the textbase
   c) the situational model
   d) none of the above

28. The type of memory representation that is most strongly established in memory

   a) is the surface form.
   b) is the textbase.
   c) is the situational model.
   d)* depends on the nature of the text and the goal behind reading it.

29. In which group would you expect a very high correlation between listening comprehension and reading comprehension?

   a) six-to-ten-year-olds
   b)* adults
   c) dyslexic readers
   d) none of the above

30. Which of the following is an example of a "Matthew effect"?

   a) Bill had a great deal of difficulty with word recognition as a young child, but with intervention he has become a skilled reader.
   b) Janice caught on to spelling-sound correspondence early on, but when reading instruction shifted to understanding whole passages, she fell behind.
   c) Tammy has always been about one year behind her peers in reading skill.
   d)* Joe was frustrated early on in reading instruction, so he avoided reading, and now he lacks many higher level comprehension skills.

31. According to Perfetti's verbal efficiency theory,

    a)   all reading problems are forms of dyslexia.
    b)   what seem to be reading problems are actually deficits of spoken and written language comprehension.
    c)   most reading problems come from deficits in working memory capacity.
    d)*   comprehension problems most often stem from inefficient lexical processing.

32. In Gernsbacher's structure-building framework, poor comprehenders are believed to form too many poorly integrated parts of the mental representation of a text. Gernsbacher has obtained evidence that this problem may result from

    a)   low working-memory capacity.
    b)*   difficulty with inhibition of irrelevant activation.
    c)   slow lexical access.
    d)   all of the above.

33. A low capacity for manipulating information in working memory is most likely to affect which of the following comprehension processes?

    a)   lexical access
    b)   inhibition of the irrelevant meaning of an ambiguous word
    c)   understanding a spoken word
    d)*   locating the referent for a pronoun that occurs several sentences after its antecedent

Integrative Essay Questions

1. What are the three types of mental representations of text that are described in construction-integration theory? About which of these representations do minimalist and constructivist theorists disagree most strongly? Explain.

2. Distinguish between local and global coherence. What language-specific mechanisms allow us to maintain each type of coherence? What general cognitive mechanisms are implicated in the maintenance of each type of coherence?

3. Compare and contrast the organizational schemes of narrative and expository texts. For which type of text are we most likely to make elaborative inferences? What evidence supports your answer?

4. Steve is a fifth-grader reading two years below his grade level. If verbal efficiency theory is correct, what tasks could you use to identify the source of Steve's reading problem? How would your choice of tasks differ from the structure-building view?

Copyright © Houghton Mifflin Company. All rights reserved.

Chapter 9
Language Production and Conversation

Keeping an Eye on the Big Picture

As Herb Clark eloquently pointed out in a recent paper on the "Dogmas of Understanding" (Clark, 1997), the complexities of language lead us to study isolated bits of the processes under rarefied conditions, but ultimately we can be misled by our simplifications if we are not careful. In particular, the social features of language use are easily ignored as we study lexical access, syntactic parsing, or grammatical planning. Yet, it is possible that all of these processes are greatly affected by the social conventions and pragmatics of conversation. This chapter affords the opportunity to examine how processing is influenced by such natural contexts. To keep the chapter manageable, I stressed the process of production, particularly the hypothesis that production has a modular organization. However, you may wish to discuss this information in class in the context of what the data suggest about the comprehension processes of the listener, as well. Thus, it is possible to use this chapter to review much of the information in Unit 2 of the text.

For example, the first part of the chapter discusses slips of the tongue and what they mean for the organization of the production system. However, it is also clear that listeners are often either forgiving of, or unaware of, slips. But it is not just that we overlook them. We overlook them in a very interesting way: we get what was meant, not what was said. To illustrate this idea you can try out the "Moses illusion" on your students (e.g., Reder & Kusbit, 1991). Particularly if placed in the context of a trivia game with several correctly constructed questions, very few people will notice a problem with the question, "How many animals of each type did Moses take on the ark?" You could have students consider a scenario in which the error in this sentence was produced unintentionally and went unnoticed by the listener. Then ask what the speech error says about production and what the listener's behavior says about comprehension. Is this an example of overly top-down processing? Does it refute the immediacy hypothesis? What happened during lexical access of the word *Moses*?

You might also note how some of the dysfluencies in normal conversations (illustrated in Table 9.1) and in any other sample of everyday conversations that the students might collect can actually be part of the useful information provided by the speaker and received by the listener. Examples of this kind of useful hesitation can be found in Clark (1996) and Clark (1997).

The Devilish Details

Speech Errors and Conversational Dysfluency

To really get a handle on the nature of speech errors and hesitations and what they imply about the production system, there really is no substitute for working through raw data. An excellent way to obtain such data is to videotape students as they do impromptu public speaking. Give each of several student volunteers a different topic to talk about, with no preparation. It is best to choose topics that the students find interesting or provocative. Film each student and have the class monitor the output for speech errors, corrections, and hesitations. These films give the students valuable practice at classifying errors and noticing patterns in dysfluency. To include the theme of what the data also mean for the comprehension system, ask the class to evaluate how confident a particular speaker was as he or she stated each idea. It will become clear that the listeners use the dysfluencies in speech to assist in understanding and evaluating a speaker's message.

Sex-Related Differences in Conversational Style

I find that a sizeable number of students have serious and persistent misconceptions about sex differences in behavior or cognitive processes. Students frequently assume that sex differences are very large, consistent, and biologically based, when in many cases sex differences are none of these. Therefore, it may be useful to accentuate the point made in the text that many of the differences in men's and women's conversational styles are not very large and they may be only loosely related to sex. In fact, there is growing consensus that the differences are more directly related to status. You may want to bring this point home by introducing students to some of the material on cross-cultural differences in conversation. For example, there is a substantial, and relatively accessible, literature on cultural differences in making requests and in the degree to which emphasis is placed on clarity or politeness (e.g., Holtgraves, 1997; Kim & Bresnahan, 1996).

Writing and Conversing

Because talking to someone else face to face seems so different from writing, it is easy for students to miss some of the connections. A way to reveal some of these connections and to illustrate some features of the planning process in writing is to have students write two brief letters, one to a close friend or parent, the other to someone not personally affiliated with the student. For example, you might have the students imagine that they have been in a minor traffic accident. Have them write two letters describing the accident, one to a friend and one to the claims adjuster for their insurance company. Ask them how the information presented changes based on the preexisting *common ground,* or lack of it, between writer and reader. Are there written equivalents of pre-sequences in the letter? What do the differences between the letters say about the planning process in writing?

Multiple Choice Test Items

1. Compared to the modern psycholinguistic view of slips of the tongue, the Freudian view relied more on the idea that

    a)   the errors are due to factors outside the language system itself.
    b)   slips reveal hidden thoughts or feelings.
    c)   slips are semantically based, not phonemically based.
    d)*   all of the above

2. If you meant to say, "I need to write a note to my brother," but instead say, "I need to write a *bote* to my *nother,*" then the error you have made should probably be considered

    a)*   an exchange error at the phonemic level.
    b)   an exchange error at the morphemic level.
    c)   an anticipation error at the syntactic level.
    d)   a perseveration error at the phonemic level.

3. The error mentioned in the previous question

    a)   is a violation of the syntactic category rule.
    b)*   exemplifies the consonant-vowel rule.
    c)   is an example of a stranding error.
    d)   all of the above

4. Which of the following represents the logical sequence of stages in speech production?

    a)   message level→syntactic level→phonemic level→morphemic level
    b)   message level→phonemic level→morphemic level→syntactic level
    c)   syntactic level→phonemic level→morphemic level→message level
    d)*   none of the above.

5. Of the following, which is a good source of evidence that utterances involve planning before generation?

    a)*   anticipation errors
    b)   perseveration errors
    c)   addition errors
    d)   all of the above

Copyright © Houghton Mifflin Company. All rights reserved.

6. Which of the following speech errors is more likely given that the person intended to say "happily married?"

      a)*   mappily harried
      b)   happied marrily
      c)   happied married
      d)   all are equally likely

7. According to the syntactic category rule, which of the following kinds of speech errors is more likely?

      a)   a substitution error that results from a poorly constructed syntactic frame
      b)   an exchange error that results from a poorly constructed syntactic frame
      c)   an error in which the inflection for a verb is omitted
      d)*   a substitution error in which an inappropriate noun activated in the lexicon is produced in place of the correct noun

8. People have more trouble naming a picture if a word with similar meaning is flashed on the screen at the same time. This finding suggests that

      a)   syntactic frames are created even in simple language production situations.
      b)   most speech errors occur at the phonemic level.
      c)*   items that are active in the lexicon compete for selection.
      d)   all of the above

9. In a stranding error

      a)   two inflections are exchanged with their word stems left in the proper place.
      b)*   two word stems are exchanged with their inflections left in the proper place.
      c)   a closed-class word is substituted for an open-class word.
      d)   two closed-class words, which play a syntactic role, are exchanged.

10. Which of the following is an example of a closed-class word?

      a)   she
      b)   the
      c)   of
      d)*   all of the above

11. Which of the following is an example of an open-class word?

      a)   person
      b)   cowboy
      c)   horrified
      d)*   all of the above

12. The consonant-vowel rule expresses regularities in speech errors that occur at the

   a) syntactic level.
   b) morphemic level.
   c)* phonemic level.
   d) all of the above

13. Which of the following is true regarding speech errors at the phonemic level?

   a) Many perseverations involve producing a vowel instead of a consonant.
   b)* Typically, vowels replace vowels and consonants replace consonants.
   c) Phonemes are usually only exchanged within the same word, rather than across different words.
   d) none of the above

14. The existence of the consonant-vowel rule in speech errors suggests that

   a)* the distinction between consonants and vowels is maintained within the phonological frame.
   b) most phonemic errors involve repetitions of consonant-vowel pairs.
   c) the rhyme portion of a word is more likely to be involved in slips than the onset portion.
   d) all of the above

15. Mixed errors, in which, for example, one slip can be traced to both phonological and semantic confusions

   a) are extremely rare.
   b) can only be accounted for by a modular view of speech production.
   c) can only be accounted for by an interactive view of speech production.
   d)* none of the above

16. Phonological errors in speech tend to result in real words rather than nonwords. A reason that this happens may be that

   a)* we monitor our speech output and are more likely to miss errors that result in real words.
   b) we plan speech in chunks of syllables, which makes it more likely that a word will be produced instead of a nonword.
   c) the lexicon is so large that substituting or exchanging a single phoneme tends to result in a legal word.
   d) all of the above

17. Hesitations in speech result from

   a) the attentional load of message construction.
   b) temporary inaccessibility of a lexical entry.
   c) situational factors that drain off attentional resources.
   d)* all of the above.

18. Which of the following statements regarding the relationship between articulation rate and short-term memory is true?

   a) Immediate recall is generally limited to the number of words someone can pronounce in seven seconds.
   b)* Short-term memory span varies by language because of differences among languages in rates of articulation.
   c) Articulation rate is related to verbal short-term memory but it is not related to working memory.
   d) none of the above

The next six questions refer to the following conversation:

LISA: Hey Rachel there's something I wanted to tell you
RACHEL: mhm
LISA: My brother is coming to town for a visit next week.
RACHEL: How nice
LISA: and you know, he broke up with that awful Martha *last* week
RACHEL: *how* very nice., when's he getting here?
LISA: next Monday
RACHEL Want to go shopping and help me pick out something really attractive before Monday?

19. The *personnel* in this conversation include

   a)* Lisa and Rachel only.
   b) Lisa's brother only.
   c) Lisa, her brother, and Rachel.
   d) Lisa's brother and his former girlfriend Martha.

20. Which of the following is part of the common ground in this conversation?

   a) Lisa has a brother.
   b) Rachel has a romantic interest in Lisa's brother.
   c) Lisa's brother lives out of town.
   d)* all of the above

Chapter 9

21. The last utterance by Rachel

   a)   is a break in the discourse record because it violates Grice's maxims.
   b)   is an example of code switching.
   c)* is comprehensible because of the common ground in the conversation.
   d)   is an example of a pre-closing.

22. The asterisks in the conversational fragment indicate that

   a)   the words were spoken with special emphasis.
   b)   nonverbal communication was used at the same time as the words were spoken.
   c)* the words were spoken at the same time.
   d)   there as a long pause at the point indicated.

23. Lisa's first statement in the conversation is an example of a

   a)   pre-question.
   b)* pre-announcement.
   c)   pre-invitation.
   d)   pre-request.

24. The utterances "mhm" and "how nice" that were made by Rachel serve to signal

   a)   that an intonation unit.
   b)* that a contribution has taken place in an adjacency pair.
   c)   that a discourse record has been established in the common ground.
   d)   all of the above.

25. Conversations typically consist of bursts of speech that are about one clause long. These bursts are known as

   a)   action sequences.
   b)* intonation units.
   c)   contributions.
   d)   none of the above

26. Code switching

   a)   typically occurs at major linguistic boundaries.
   b)   occurs when bilinguals switch from one language to another during a conversation
   c)   may occur when something is difficult to explain.
   d)* all of the above

Copyright © Houghton Mifflin Company. All rights reserved.

27. Intonation units

    a)   are defined as brief utterances bounded by pauses.
    b)   nearly always increase in pitch toward the end of the clause.
    c)*   reveal units of message planning by the speaker.
    d)   all of the above

28. Keesha and Chad start out talking about movies they both like, but soon they find themselves, through a string of associations, on the topic of how their friendship got started. This scenario illustrates the idea that conversations

    a)*   are locally managed.
    b)   involve lots of code switching.
    c)   sometimes fail to result in a discourse record.
    d)   none of the above

29. As a general tendency, men in conversations, compared to women, are more likely to

    a)   use adjectives.
    b)   use hedges.
    c)*   interrupt.
    d)   all of the above

30. There is growing evidence that sex differences in conversational style are linked to differences in

    a)*   status.
    b)   innate tendencies.
    c)   sensitivity to nonverbal cues.
    d)   none of the above

31. In the process of writing, *translating* refers to

    a)   formulating goals that are appropriate for the intended audience.
    b)   the idea that the act of writing can alter the writer's own knowledge base.
    c)   the process of checking one's progress toward the goals of an essay.
    d)*   the sentence generation process.

32. In writing, the translating process ____, but the processes of planning and reviewing ____.

    a)*   uses considerable attentional capacity; use even more capacity.
    b)   is relatively automatic; require considerable attentional resources.
    c)   uses the most capacity; use considerable attentional capacity.
    d)   uses considerable attentional capacity; are relatively automatic.

33. More successful writers spend more time in planning, but they are still more willing to alter their organization and revise their written product more thoroughly. These writers use a strategy known as

    a)   the reading-editing strategy.
    b)   the knowledge base strategy.
    c)*   the knowledge transforming strategy.
    d)   the knowledge telling strategy.

Integrative Essay Questions

1. Give an example of a speech error that you would regard as a mixed error. Trace through the mental processes that produced the utterance from the message level to articulation. Is your explanation based on a modular or an interactive view?

2. Give examples of two different speech errors, each one reflecting the operation of a different level of the speech production system. Why would each error be produced, based on the general model of speech production outlined in the text? Are these explanations superior to the Freudian view of slips?

3. Outline the mental processes that allow you to have a conversation with someone else. Of the processes you mentioned, which are the most demanding of your working memory resources? Justify your conclusions about working memory demands.

4. Compare and contrast the mental processes involved in having a conversation and in writing an essay. Which processes involved in writing make similar attentional demands as conversing and which make more demands?

Copyright © Houghton Mifflin Company. All rights reserved.

Chapter 10
Language Acquisition: Biological Foundations

Keeping an Eye on the Big Picture

There are so many different things going on as children acquire language that researchers have a daunting task trying to unravel the mysteries of language development. It is important to keep in mind that this area presents the same problem for the student, who can quickly become overwhelmed just trying to keep the basic milestones in mind. There are, of course, two general schemes for presenting any sort of developmental material: topically and chronologically. There is something to be said for each approach. In the text, I used a topical organizational system because it encourages students to focus on major principles and to relate the material to other parts of the book. However, chronologies can help the students get a feel for what the whole process looks like. Thus, in class I often supplement the topical approach by presenting a chronology in lecture and using it as an exercise in which the topical and chronological approaches to organization of the information are compared. For example, a useful introductory exercise for this part of the course is to present the students with a simple chronology like the one below, and ask the students to relate this chronology to major topics of the course. What milestones represent the growth of phonology? Which of them illustrate how the lexicon grows or mastery of syntax changes over time? Are there milestones that depend on combinations of these factors?

Some Milestones of Language Production

Age	Competence
one--two years	First words around age one. Names for objects before actions. Earliest action-oriented terms usually only express outcomes of actions (e.g. "broken"; "dirty")
two--three years	Two-word utterances, then gradually increasing use of inflections and function words Indication of cause-effect (e.g. "eat all gone") Use terms for salient perceptual attributes: "Big-small" precedes "tall-short" "high-low" which precede "wide-narrow" Terms for the possessive and for functions (e.g., "my truck"; "dump truck") Location and orientation terms: "in"; "on"; "under"; "top"; "bottom"

Copyright © Houghton Mifflin Company. All rights reserved.

three--four years   Appropriate use of causal terms (e.g., "if"; "because")
Mastery of temporal terms:
"now/then" and "before/after" precedes "today/yesterday/tomorrow"
More location and orientation terms:
"front/back"; "above/below" (these often take until four or five years of age)

The milestones given above are merely some representative samples, but by considering what kinds of changes are reflected in these or other major milestones, you can set the class up for considering how particular areas of language develop over time. These considerations lead quite naturally into the major question posed in the chapter: To what extent does the developmental progression depend on innate factors?

The Devilish Details

Constraints and Bootstrapping

Various explanations of language development phenomena rely heavily on the concept of (possibly innate) constraints and how such initial knowledge can be used via bootstrapping to make the most effective use of language input. To give the students a feel for how useful constraints can be, you can put your students in a situation in which they get unfamiliar language input and try to make some sense out of it. For example, you could have the students try to interpret the first stanza of the classic children's poem, *"Jabberwocky"*:

> Twas brillig, and the slithy toves
> Did gyre and gimble in the wabe:
> All mimsy were the borogoves
> And the Mome raths outgrabe.

The students' attempts to make sense of this stanza will include examples of trying to use knowledge of syntax to determine the part of speech of a word, as a way of making a guess about its meaning. Many students will not even realize that they are making assumptions about parts of speech until you point it out to them. This exercise puts the students, to some degree, in the child's place, but it is important to point out the advantages they have in a game like this in comparison to a toddler acquiring a native language. These advantages make it all the more clear how remarkable native language acquisition really is and why much of the early acquisition process may depend on innate knowledge.

By the way, if your students are interested in the "right" interpretation of "Jabberwocky", they can check out the very charming "Jabberwocky home page" at:

http://sar.usf.edu/~zazuetaa/jabberwocky/start.html

Mean Length of Utterance (MLU)

There really is no substitute for considering actual language samples. Written transcripts of children's speech are useful, but I always try to give the students some exposure to the full messy stimulus, actual speech samples. One of the things I have students try to do with such samples is to analyze them in terms of MLU. It soon becomes clear to the students that the measure is useful, but somewhat simplistic. Furthermore, there are some subtleties to deriving the measure. They will face, as Roger Brown and his colleagues did, some questions of how to calculate some forms. For example:

- What should you do when a word is repeated? Brown counted repeated attempts at pronouncing a word as only a single production. However, if a word was repeated for emphasis (e.g., *"No no no!"*), then each word was counted.
- How should you count compound words (e.g., *birthday*) and reduplications that seem to be a single word to the child (e.g., *night-night*)? Brown counted them as single morphemes.
- Obviously, inflections such as –s for plural count as a morpheme, but what about productions like *gonna* or *hafta*? Brown counted these as one morpheme because they seem to function that way for the children in his study.

Once some utterances have been used for calculating MLUs for children of different ages, it is useful to see what else is progressing in these utterances besides length. What is happening to vocabulary? What kinds of syntactic forms are seen only later in development?

Multiple Choice Test Items

1. If we compare young children's comprehension and production of language, it is clear that

    a) comprehension and production proceed together at about the same level of competence.
    b) children tend to use words before they understand them, so production runs ahead of comprehension.
    c) we must infer comprehension ability from production ability, so the two cannot be separated.
    d)* children tend to understand words before they can produce them.

2. When the high-amplitude sucking procedure is used to study infants' speech perception, researchers are primarily interested in whether

    a) infants will habituate to a sound that is repeated over and over.
    b) sucking rate will increase when a familiar sound is presented.
    c)* infants will pay more attention as the speech sound that is being played is changed.
    d) all of the above.

Copyright © Houghton Mifflin Company. All rights reserved.

3. In the conditioned head turn procedure, the child is conditioned to

   a) turn his head toward the location of a hidden toy whenever he hears a sound that he recognizes.
   b) turn his head when he recognizes a parent's voice rather than a stranger's voice.
   c) look toward the person speaking whenever a novel sound is produced.
   d)* turn his head toward the location of a hidden toy whenever the sound that is being played changes.

4. An important limitation of diary studies for understanding language production is that

   a) the adult may write down interpretations of what was heard rather than exactly what the child said.
   b) a biased sample of utterances may be obtained.
   c) only the more unusual utterances may be recorded because they seem more notable.
   d)* all of the above

5. The "wug test" used in Berko's (1958) classic research is an example of studying language development through

   a)* elicited production.
   b) diary recordings.
   c) cases of feral children.
   d) the high amplitude sucking procedure.

6. Studying cases of feral children, such as the "Wild Boy of Aveyron"

   a) generally reveals that such children start off slowly but soon catch up in language acquisition.
   b) provides strong support for a critical period of language acquisition.
   c) demonstrates that language acquisition need not move in step with general cognitive development.
   d)* none of the above

7. The concept of a critical period includes the idea that

   a) language acquisition will be difficult if there is not adequate language experience before middle childhood.
   b) there is a maturational component to language acquisition.
   c) language acquisition is based largely on innate mechanisms.
   d)* all of the above

Chapter 10

8. Which of the following statements is true?

   a)* By age five a child's brain has reached nearly its full adult weight.
   b) Myelinization, which increases the efficiency of neural transmission, occurs mainly in prenatal development.
   c) Language acquisition and brain maturation are uncorrelated, supporting the idea that language acquisition is not a maturational process.
   d) none of the above.

9. Which of the following statements is true?

   a) The ability to perceive distinctions among speech sounds, such as /ba/ and /pa/, first appears between one and two years of age.
   b) Children can perceive the difference between two speech sounds only when they can produce the two sounds.
   c)* Infants do not need to have heard two speech sounds used in their native language in order to perceive the distinction between them.
   d) none of the above.

10. From six to twelve months of age, perception of speech contrasts that are *not* used in an infant's native language

   a) is completely absent.
   b)* gets worse.
   c) gets better.
   d) cannot yet be tested.

11. When infants make the same sound over and over, as in [dadada],

   a) it is called variegated babbling.
   b)* it is called reduplicated babbling.
   c) they are attempting to say a word.
   d) none of the above

12. Infant babbling

   a) is unaffected by the language environment.
   b) nearly always involves saying the same syllable over and over.
   c) is not observed among children who are born deaf.
   d)* none of the above

Copyright © Houghton Mifflin Company. All rights reserved.

13. The ability to recognize that the same vowel sound appears with two different consonants, as in /bi/ and /di/,

    a)   is present within the first few months of life.
    b)   cannot be tested with the high-amplitude sucking procedure.
    c)*   depends on language experience.
    d)   is an example of an innate language ability.

14. According to the prosodic bootstrapping hypothesis,

    a)   sensitivity to prosody develops around the end of the first year.
    b)   breaks between words are used to help infants learn the prosody of their native language.
    c)*   regular patterns of stress and intonation help infants determine word boundaries.
    d)   all of the above.

15. Which of the following is true regarding child-directed speech?

    a)   It uses exaggerated intonation and very clear articulation.
    b)   It may be of help to infants trying to understand speech segmentation.
    c)   It is only a rough guide to word boundaries in a sentence.
    d)*   all of the above

16. Which of the following statements about early lexical development is true?

    a)   At one year, infants can perceive the difference between familiar and unfamiliar sounds but not the difference between familiar and unfamiliar words.
    b)   Before ten months of age, infants can only perceive groups of sounds as familiar if the grouping is set off by distinct pauses.
    c)*   Even before age one, infants can recognize that a particular word within a sentence is familiar.
    d)   none of the above

17. By two years of age, children

    a)   may use more than a hundred different words.
    b)   understand more words than they can produce.
    c)   are using word combinations to express ideas.
    d)*   all of the above

Chapter 10

18. Cathy, who is almost two, sees a rabbit for the first time and says "Kitty!" This is an example of

    a) underextension.
    b)* overextension.
    c) semantic bootstrapping.
    d) telegraphic speech.

19. A young child who says "*Nink!*" to indicate that she wants a drink has displayed

    a) underextension.
    b) overextension.
    c)* a holophrase.
    d) telegraphic speech.

20. You pass by a pet store with a young child. When the child is drawn toward a puppy, you point at it and say "doggie." The child is likely to assume that "doggie"

    a) refers to the puppy itself, not the whole situation.
    b) refers to the puppy and other things of the same type.
    c) is the only appropriate one for dogs.
    d)* all of the above

21. You show a three-year-old a picture of someone working in a field with an unfamiliar tool, and you say that this person is "*trabbing.*" The child is likely to realize that *trabbing* refers to the action depicted, not the tool itself. The child has made use of

    a) semantic bootstrapping.
    b)* syntactic bootstrapping.
    c) the taxonomic assumption.
    d) the mutual exclusivity assumption.

22. Which of the following is an example of the telegraphic speech typical of children around a year and a half to two years of age?

    a) happy more
    b) Mommy not go now
    c)* more juice
    d) all of the above

23. Mean length of utterance is usually measured in ___ per utterance.

    a) words
    b) syllables
    c)* morphemes
    d) phonemes

Copyright © Houghton Mifflin Company. All rights reserved.

24. A typical mean length of utterance for a three-year-old would be around

    a)   4.5 to 5.0.
    b)*   3.0 to 3.5.
    c)   1.5 to 2.0.
    d)   none of the above

25. Observations of parent-child conversations show that children's acquisition of syntactic rules

    a)   depends almost exclusively on innate factors.
    b)   is based on parental approval for approximating correct grammar.
    c)*   proceeds with little or no feedback about what is grammatical.
    d)   begins with systematic grammatical training at about three years of age.

26. Theories of grammar acquisition that start with the assumption that children have innate knowledge of syntactic categories are known as

    a)   discontinuous theories.
    b)*   continuous theories.
    c)   PDP theories.
    d)   none of the above

27. Discovering which words in your language are nouns and which are verbs might proceed by using semantic properties of words in the context to map a specific word onto its syntactic category. This process is known as

    a)   overregularization.
    b)   parameter setting.
    c)   syntactic bootstrapping.
    d)*   semantic bootstrapping.

28. Which of the following is an example of a parameter in the sense used by Chomsky?

    a)*   A given language has either a fixed word order or a variable word order.
    b)   Languages have the least restrictive grammar possible.
    c)   All languages have a syntactic category for *things* and another category for *actions*.
    d)   all of the above

29. According to the subset principle, a parameter should have an initial setting that corresponds to

    a)   the value used in the majority of the world's languages.
    b)   the value used in the fewest languages.
    c)*   the value that leads to the most restrictive grammar.
    d)   the value that leads to the least restrictive grammar.

Chapter 10

30. In PRO-drop languages

    a)   there are no pronouns.
    b)   the subject of the sentence follows the verb.
    c)*   having an explicit subject is optional.
    d)   the null subject parameter is set initially at "not optional."

31. If you trace the developmental progression of the correct use of both regular and irregular verb forms, you find that correct usage

    a)   increases steadily over time.
    b)   increases slowly and then accelerates.
    c)   increases quickly, levels off, then increases again.
    d)*   none of the above

32. Using terms like "goed" or "taked" are examples of

    a)   holophrases.
    b)   telegraphic speech.
    c)   overextension.
    d)*   overregularization.

33. According to the blocking principle,

    a)   children extend new words to objects from the same taxonomic category.
    b)   children have innate knowledge that some verb forms are irregular.
    c)   knowing that the past tense is signaled by the inflection *–d* blocks production of words like *went*.
    d)*   knowledge of irregular forms like *went* block the production of forms like *goed*.

34. According to McClelland and Rumelhart's (1986) PDP model of acquisition of verb forms,

    a)*   no innate principles are needed to explain overregularization.
    b)   blocking is based on innate negative connection weights.
    c)   children initially learn regular forms and then start to learn irregular forms.
    d)   overregularization is based on occasional memory failures.

Integrative Essay Questions

1. Describe the *gavagai problem* and its connection to the problem of explaining lexical development. In what sense is the problem compounded by the lack of negative evidence in language acquisition?

2. Describe how a specific experiment could be designed to determine if ten-month-old infants have

Copyright © Houghton Mifflin Company. All rights reserved.

lost the ability to recognize speech contrasts that they could perceive at six months of age.

3. Compare and contrast parameter-setting and processing-load explanations for the tendency to omit subjects in telegraphic speech.

4. Compare and contrast prosodic bootstrapping, syntactic bootstrapping, and semantic bootstrapping. Could all of these be used by the same child during language acquisition? Explain.

5. Contrast Pinker's explanation for overregularization, which has an innate component, with McClelland and Rumelhart's explanation, which has no innate component.

Chapter 11
Language Acquisition in Special Circumstances

Keeping an Eye on the Big Picture

The big picture, in this case, refers in part to the idea that we can examine atypical development to determine where the seams are in the connections between language and cognition. In addition to second-language acquisition and the acquisition of sign language, the chapter covers several developmental problems that affect the development of language and/or cognitive abilities. In this regard, I think it is important to stress one other aspect of the big picture: namely, that children with the disorders discussed in the chapter are not just interesting cases for scientists to consider; they are, first, foremost, and always, people. I do not see any inherent inconsistency, however, between stressing their importance to the study of psycholinguistics and stressing their humanity. In both cases we gain insight by looking at how the strengths and weaknesses of these children influence, and are influenced by, their everyday lives. Accordingly, I find it useful to expose my students to information about the everyday experiences of children who have disorders that are important to the study of psycholinguistics.

Even in a relatively rural setting, like mine here at Washington State University, it is not difficult to find professionals and parents who work with children with Down syndrome or with severe language delays. Such guest speakers can often give valuable information and a more fleshed-out picture of special needs children than the students could ever get from a textbook. In addition, there are a number of good resources on the Internet that provide not only basic information but also pictures, stories, and artwork that help complete the picture of what children with various disorders are really like, as people. A couple of the many good sites to explore are:

http://www.nas.com/downsyn/information.html

This site has articles and answers to frequently asked questions about Down syndrome.

http://www.williams-syndrome.org/

This is the Web page for the Williams Syndrome Association. It provides a good introduction to this rare, but fascinating, disorder.

You may also wish to expand on the book's coverage by including a discussion of autism. Because of the pervasiveness of the developmental problems in autism, and because of the poorly understood nature of the disorder, it is more difficult to draw conclusions regarding language-cognition relations from the study of autism than from some other examples of atypical development. However, it is certainly possible to use a discussion of autism to focus on the reciprocal relationship between language development and social development. In addition, a discussion of echolalia can be used to illustrate how typical language development depends on children's sensitivity to duality of patterning. You might also point out that echolalia demonstrates a limitation of MLUs for comparing the level of language development across children. Some good resources for autism information are available on the Web, for example:

> http://info.med.yale.edu/chldstdy/autism/
> http://web.syr.edu/~jmwobus/autism/

The Devilish Details

Sign Language

Misconceptions about sign language abound, and most often the misconceptions center on the belief that sign language is just an elaborate form of communication with iconic gestures. To elaborate on the discussion of this issue in the text, you may find it useful to invite someone fluent in sign into your class to demonstrate aspects of the grammar of ASL. If this is not possible, you can show a film of someone communicating in sign and ask the students to try to interpret it based just on the gestures they see. For example, Gleason (1997) suggested viewing conversations from the movie *Children of a Lesser God* with the sound turned off. Some information can be gleaned from just watching these conversations, but most of it comes from context and facial expressions, which are, of course, also available when we interpret spoken language. Watching such clips does make it clear that sign language goes well beyond a set of standardized gestures.

Bilingualism

Unless your students tend to be bilingual, or have contact with many bilingual people, it may be difficult for them to appreciate the developmental pattern of gaining proficiency in a second language. You might have them interview several bilingual people or have bilingual guests come to class to be interviewed. One of the interesting questions to discuss with the guests is the age at which they were exposed to the second language. How is this reflected in the presence or absence of an accent? Also, the students might wish to ask when the person began to "think in the second language." Most bilinguals will readily discuss their phenomenological experience of thinking in a second language. The class can then discuss what this phrase might really mean in terms of the relations between language and thought that have been discussed throughout the course.

Dissociations and Modules

Students (and many professionals!) tend to fall easily into the trap of using dissociation evidence in a very simplistic fashion. As is discussed in the text, the controversy over the nature of "specific language impairment" shows that it is necessary to perform a rather fine-grained analysis of the cognitive and linguistic skills involved in a dissociation before concluding that we have specific modules that can be selectively damaged. This can also be illustrated nicely with Williams syndrome. A recent, and very readable, article by Lenhoff, Wang, Greenberg, and Belugi (1997) published in *Scientific American* makes it clear that it is essential to include cross-language comparisons in studies of disorders such as Williams syndrome before drawing the conclusion that language abilities are preserved. It is important to get the general implications of this idea across to the students here because it will prepare them for the final chapter of the text, which tells the story of the study of aphasia. The history of aphasia research is largely a tale of an overly simplistic interpretation of dissociation evidence.

Multiple Choice Test Items

1. The rudimentary communication system developed when people who speak different languages must live together is known as a

    a) source language.
    b) home-sign system.
    c) creole.
    d)* pidgin.

2. A creole is

    a) a dialect of an established language.
    b)* invented by the children of speakers of a pidgin.
    c) based completely on a bioprogram rather than on language experience.
    d) none of the above.

3. One piece of evidence that supports the critical period hypothesis regarding language-acquisition is that

    a)* children, but not adults, invent creoles.
    b) children, but not adults, invent pidgins.
    c) children acquire a second language most fluently only if their initial exposure to the second language occurs by age two.
    d) all of the above.

4. According to Bickerton's language bioprogram hypothesis,

    a) an innate grammar allows for the invention of a pidgin.
    b)* an innate grammar allows for the invention of a creole.
    c) most creoles are syntactically related to English.
    d) creoles share the word-order pattern of the dominant language of the region.

Copyright © Houghton Mifflin Company. All rights reserved.

5. Children who grow up in a home in which two different languages are each used frequently

   a)   never show any sign of confusing the two languages.
   b)   will first acquire one of the languages and then will start to acquire the other.
   c)   do not learn either language as well as a child brought up in a monolingual home.
   d)* will be able to acquire both languages in a typically developing fashion.

6. If we examine second language acquisition by age of exposure to the second language, we find that

   a)   early in the course of acquisition adults have an advantage.
   b)   mastery of the grammar of the second language is best if exposure occurs before adulthood.
   c)   young children may take months to attempt to speak the second language.
   d)* all of the above

7. Some investigators believe that there are multiple critical periods in language acquisition. For example, age six may be the end of a critical period for mastery of ____, but the end of the critical period for the mastery of ____ is probably several years later.

   a)* phonology; syntax
   b)   syntax; semantics
   c)   syntax; pragmatics
   d)   comprehension; production

8. According to the *competition model* of second-language acquisition, the interference between the primary language and the second language

   a)   is unrelated to how fully the primary language has been mastered.
   b)* increases with age of first exposure to the second language.
   c)   is due to inappropriate use of default settings in the innate grammar.
   d)   all of the above

9. Let's say that your friend Gunther is a native speaker of German, but also speaks English pretty well. You give him the following "sentence" and ask him who is performing the action: *The vegetable eat the fruits.* Gunther reasons that the fruits are doing the eating. He seems to have relied on

   a)   word order.
   b)   animacy.
   c)* subject-verb agreement.
   d)   all of the cues equally.

10. A reasonable overall conclusion regarding the implications of the evidence on second-language acquisition for the nativist hypothesis is that

    a)   there must be some kind of innately determined critical period.
    b)   interference between languages occurs without any influence of innate knowledge.
    c)   only the principles and parameters view accounts for the whole pattern of results.
    d)*   the data are generally consistent with the nativist hypothesis, but other explanations are viable, too.

11. The developmental course of sign-language acquisition

    a)   is analogous to spoken language acquisition if the parents are fluent in sign.
    b)   is delayed, and final levels of fluency potentially compromised if there is a substantial delay in beginning to learn sign.
    c)   may be influenced by innate factors in a similar fashion as spoken language.
    d)*   all of the above

12. If we compare the nature of sign language and spoken language we find that

    a)   they have comparable expressive power, but only spoken languages have duality of patterning.
    b)   because sign language is based on movement, its grammar has more expressive power than languages based on vocalization.
    c)   each sign language is an intricate system for translating a particular spoken language, such as English in the case of ASL, into a series of movements.
    d)*   none of the above.

13. In sign language, the primes

    a)   are the set of gestures that correspond to the vocabulary of the language.
    b)*   play the same role in sign language that phonemes play in spoken language.
    c)   play the same role in sign language that inflections play in spoken language.
    d)   are basic features of a sign that reflect differences in hand configuration.

14. The term *home-sign* refers to

    a)   the first set of signs that a deaf child acquires, generally the signs for mother, father, eat, and drink.
    b)   the gestural system invented by hearing parents to try to communicate with their deaf child.
    c)*   the gestural system invented by deaf children to try to communicate with their hearing parents.
    d)   the sign-language equivalent of a creole language.

15. Studies of deaf children who experience delayed exposure to sign language

   a)* support the hypothesis that we have a biological predisposition for language.
   b) provide proof for the principles and parameters theory.
   c) provide evidence against the idea of a critical period.
   d) none of the above.

16. According to the "less-is-more hypothesis,"

   a) developmental improvements in information-processing ability allow for improved ability to acquire language.
   b)* developmental improvements in information-processing ability can make some aspects of language acquisition more difficult.
   c) the less language ability an infant has developed, the more his or her maturation focuses on the development of other cognitive abilities.
   d) the less strongly developed a primary language is, the more language capacity remains to acquire a second language.

17. According to a strongly nativist view of acquisition, if we examine the language abilities and general cognitive abilities of children, we should find that

   a)* the two kinds of abilities can be dissociated.
   b) children with high cognitive ability will also have high language ability.
   c) children with high cognitive ability must have low language ability.
   d) none of the above

18. Which of the following would be an example of a double dissociation?

   a)* You identify children with high language ability and low cognitive ability and other children with low language ability and high cognitive ability.
   b) You identify children with high language ability and low cognitive ability, but all children with low language ability have low cognitive ability.
   c) You identify children with high language ability and high cognitive ability and other children with low language ability and low cognitive ability.
   d) all of the above.

19. Children diagnosed with the disorder known as *specific language impairment* have

   a) problems mastering the grammar of their native language.
   b) trouble with processing some auditory signals.
   c) slower speed of information processing than their same-age peers.
   d)* all of the above

Chapter 11

20. Children with Down syndrome

   a) have normal IQs but very deficient language skills.
   b)* often have significant mental retardation without major disruption of their ability to acquire the basic grammar of their language.
   c) tend to have significant mental retardation, delayed language acquisition, and severe problems with syntax.
   d) develop completely normal language proficiency even if their level of mental retardation is severe.

21. In the chatterbox syndrome,

   a) a child with early and intensive language training develops unusually high language skill.
   b) a child with mental retardation talks excessively and displays poorly developed grammatical skill.
   c)* a child has mental retardation but is very fluent in language and displays well-developed grammatical skill.
   d) none of the above

22. Jack speaks fluently and has a relatively good vocabulary considering that his IQ has been tested at 55. He performs especially poorly on tests that require visual spatial ability or logical reasoning. Jack fits the pattern of people with

   a) Down syndrome.
   b) chatterbox syndrome.
   c) specific language impairment.
   d)* Williams syndrome.

23. Tests of whether the major cognitive milestones in Piaget's theory of cognitive development serve as prerequisites for particular language competencies have revealed that

   a) understanding the concept of conservation is necessary for mastery of the use of passives.
   b) language competencies are prerequisites for cognitive advancement, not the other way around.
   c) many language-acquisition problems can be traced to failure to achieve specific cognitive milestones.
   d)* none of the above

24. Overall, the evidence from studies of mental retardation and language acquisition show that

   a)* some children show a high degree of grammatical competence despite significant mental retardation.
   b) children with significant language-acquisition problems also have mental retardation.
   c) syntactic processing is modular, but semantic processing is not.
   d) all of the above

Integrative Essay Questions

1. Outline the most important evidence for the existence of one or more critical periods in language acquisition. Next, contrast two different interpretations of this evidence. Is it possible to explain the data without appealing to a nativist view of language acquisition?

2. Compare the situations faced by a child reared in an environment in which a pidgin is the dominant language with the situation faced by a deaf child born to parents who know no sign language. Does either of these situations provide convincing evidence in support of a nativist view of language acquisition? Explain.

3. Explain the concept of a double dissociation. What evidence have you learned about that represents the strongest case for a double dissociation between language and more general cognitive abilities? Justify your answer.

4. Studies of children with specific language impairment, Williams syndrome, and Down syndrome have been interpreted as showing a dissociation between language and cognition. What are the problems with such a strong interpretation of these data? Give an example of how a more fine grained analysis of the abilities have weakened the support for a strongly nativist view.

Chapter 12
Language and the Localization of Function

Keeping an Eye on the Big Picture

The main lesson from the previous chapter was that what seems to be a straightforward interpretation of an apparent dissociation can be misleading. Only a fine-grained examination of both language and cognition can justify strong conclusions at the implementation level of analysis. This theme carries over into the final chapter of the text. Thus, to augment the classic maxim, I want students to see that "there is nothing so practical as a good theory *of function*." In the last chapter of the text, I present the history of research on brain-language relations organized around the key idea that the models in this domain of research made great strides when theories and data from linguistics and psycholinguistics were integrated with physiological data.

The study of brain-language relations is one of the areas in which it is most evident that physiological researchers have benefited from guidance provided by theories of function. To have a good model of localization of function, you have to have a good idea of what functions to localize. Although the point seems obvious when stated that way, in practice the "sexiness" of new research using PET scans and fMRI technology can sometimes blind people to the importance of the research of the type discussed in the first eleven chapters of the text. The point I try to get my students to see is that, as wonderful, even revolutionary, as these new tools are, they become much more powerful when the researcher is guided by a good theory of the nature of the functions to be localized.

In terms of helping the students get a better understanding of how well the new tools themselves are used, there are a number of excellent resources available on the Internet. A few great sites for getting a close look at brain images in both normal and injured or diseased brains include:

(1) The Whole Brain Atlas, which can be found at:
http://www.med.harvard.edu:80/AANLIB/home.html

(2) Neuroscience Links, which can be found at:
http://www.tbi.pmr.vcu.edu/neuro.htm

(3) Brain Imaging Demos, which can be found at:
http://www.bic.mni.mcgill.ca/demos/

The Devilish Details

The Dynamics of Brain Injury

A misconception that students sometimes form when learning about brain injuries is that the lesion and its consequences are static. Of course, what really happens is that there are changes over time at the lesion site and changes in how the person is affected. Both the dynamics of lesions and their consequences are wonderfully illustrated in the Whole Brain Atlas site noted above. Imaging data for a variety of lesions, including some that resulted in aphasia, are shown. In addition, physical changes in the brains are shown over time, and these can be viewed as a "movie." The student can also select slices at different depths, which is wonderful for helping the student think of the lesions in three dimensions rather than two. Students can learn a lot about the recovery process by exploring the website of the National Aphasia Association. The URL for the site is:

http://www.aphasia.org/

In particular the section on rehabilitation research gives a good feel for the dynamics of recovery and the connection between research and practice.

Imaging Studies, Lesion Studies, and Causality

Another important point that often escapes students is the complementary nature of studies that trace activity in the normal brain given different tasks and studies that look at deficits in processing after brain damage. The idea that activation studies of normal brains are important to show that lesion studies are generalizable to the normal brain is not hard to grasp. In contrast, it is easy to overlook the fact that studies of brain activity during task performance are, in essence, correlational studies. Lesion studies provide important complementary evidence that the brain area in question is *necessary* to a particular process. An analogy may help. Let's say that we measured the activation of the musculature for the larynx as people tried to memorize a list of words. We would find increased activity in these muscles compared to a condition in which the participants were told to merely look at the words. These data show that the larynx is the processing site for memorization, right? Of course not! The data would show only that some people were using speech codes in memorization. We certainly wouldn't expect that someone who lost the ability to speak would lose the ability to memorize a list. What is not so obvious to many students is that an analogous error in logic is made if we draw firm conclusions about localization of function merely from data that show an area of increased brain activation during a certain mental task.

Chapter 12

Multiple Choice Test Items

1. Which of the following expresses the relationship between the terms *aphasia* and *anomia*?

    a)* Aphasia is a more general term for language disturbance while anomia refers more specifically to problems with retrieving words.
    b)   Anomia is a more general term for language disturbance while aphasia refers more specifically to problems with retrieving words.
    c)   Aphasia refers to a disturbance of comprehension while anomia refers to a disturbance of production.
    d)   Anomia refers to a disturbance of comprehension while aphasia refers to a disturbance of production.

2. Broca's area is located

    a)   in the left temporal lobe.
    b)   just above the angular gyrus.
    c)* in the left frontal lobe.
    d)   diffusely throughout the right hemisphere.

3. Wernicke's area is located

    a)* in the left temporal lobe.
    b)   just above the angular gyrus.
    c)   in the left frontal lobe.
    d)   diffusely throughout the right hemisphere.

4. Paul Broca's studies of the patient Leborgne led to the idea that

    a)   speech abilities are localized in the left temporal lobe.
    b)* speech abilities are localized in the left frontal lobe.
    c)   comprehension abilities are localized in the left temporal lobe.
    d)   comprehension abilities are localized in the left frontal lobe.

5. Paul Broca's studies of Leborgne and other aphasic patients suggested that

    a)   a disturbance of speaking ability could result from rather localized brain damage.
    b)   the two hemispheres of the brain are not functionally identical.
    c)   expressive language ability is localized in an area of the left frontal lobe.
    d)* all of the above.

Copyright © Houghton Mifflin Company. All rights reserved.

6. Which set of early investigators are most closely associated with warning that views of strictly localized language functions may be misleadingly oversimplified?

    a)   Wernicke and Freud
    b)   Head and Lichtheim
    c)   Freud and Lichtheim
    d)*   Freud and Head

7. Jack has damage to the arcuate fasciculus. His most obvious problem is a difficulty with speech repetition. He fits the classic description of a patient with _____ aphasia.

    a)   Broca's
    b)   Wernicke's
    c)*   conduction
    d)   global

8. June has damage in the left frontal lobe. Her speech is not fluent but her language comprehension seems relatively undisturbed. She fits the classic description of a patient with _____ aphasia.

    a)*   Broca's
    b)   Wernicke's
    c)   conduction
    d)   global

9. Carlos has damage in the frontal and temporal regions of his left hemisphere. He is not fluent and also has obvious difficulties with language comprehension. He fits the classic description of a patient with _____ aphasia.

    a)   Broca's
    b)   Wernicke's
    c)   conduction
    d)*   global

10. Imelda has damage in the left temporal lobe. Her speech is fluent but her language comprehension is poor. She fits the classic description of a patient with _____ aphasia.

    a)   Broca's
    b)*   Wernicke's
    c)   conduction
    d)   global

Chapter 12

11. If you wanted to determine the specific site of a brain lesion in a living patient and you had your choice of all the available technologies, which of the following would be the best to use?

    a)   EEG
    b)   CT scanning
    c)*   MRI
    d)   PET scanning

12. If you wanted to determine the area of the brain that is active as a normal volunteer performs a particular mental task and you had your choice of all the available technologies, which of the following would be the best to use?

    a)   EEG
    b)   CT scanning
    c)   MRI
    d)*   PET scanning

13. Which of the following techniques is based on X-rays?

    a)   PET scans
    b)*   CT scans
    c)   fMRI
    d)   all of the above

14. Professor Smith is using sensors on the scalp to record the changes in the electrical activity of the brain as a person hears language stimuli. Dr. Smith is looking for changes in ___ over time.

    a)   fMRI pictures
    b)   CT scans
    c)   PET scans
    d)*   event-related potentials

15. Dr. Jones has a patient whose CT scan shows several small scattered lesions, none of which occur in the left frontal lobe. A PET scan reveals abnormally low activity in the left frontal lobe, even though there appears to be no damage in that region. This patient

    a)   will not show Broca's aphasia symptoms because Broca's area is not damaged.
    b)*   may show Broca's aphasia symptoms even if Broca's area is not damaged.
    c)   has language functions localized in the right hemisphere.
    d)   shows an impossible pattern, so one of the tests has been interpreted incorrectly.

Copyright © Houghton Mifflin Company. All rights reserved.

16. Comparing the results of a large number of studies of the effects of lesions on language and those of electrical stimulation of the brain lead us to the idea that

    a)   there are people for whom the right hemisphere is dominant for language.
    b)   there is considerable variability as to what language functions are controlled by particular brain areas.
    c)   some individuals do not have one hemisphere that is dominant for language.
    d)*   all of the above.

17. Studies using PET scan data during lexical processing have shown that

    a)   Wernicke's area is activated whenever words are processed semantically.
    b)   lexical access is a completely frontal lobe process.
    c)*   whether Wernicke's area is activated depends on what kind of lexical task is performed.
    d)   both Broca's and Wernicke's areas are activated when nonwords are processed, but only Wernicke's area is activated when processing real words.

18. Acquired dyslexia can result from damage to

    a)   Wernicke's area.
    b)   Broca's area.
    c)*   either Broca's or Wernicke's area.
    d)   none of the above.

The next four questions refer to the following (hypothetical) cases. Jim has fluent speech but experiences great difficulty reading. He has particular problems with function words and with pronouncing and understanding less common words. Like Jim, Jane has fluent speech but experiences great difficulty reading. Unlike Jim, she has particular problems with words that are exceptions to the usual phonological rules. In addition, she seems to have to pronounce a word in order to understand its meaning.

19. Jim is most likely to be diagnosed with

    a)   Broca's aphasia.
    b)   Wernicke's aphasia.
    c)   surface dyslexia.
    d)*   deep dyslexia.

Chapter 12   113

20. From the information presented, you would predict that Jim has damage in which area(s) of the brain?

   a)*   left frontal and parietal areas
   b)   diffusely throughout the right hemisphere
   c)   left temporal area
   d)   either the left or the right occipital areas

21. Jane is most likely to be diagnosed with

   a)   Broca's aphasia.
   b)   Wernicke's aphasia.
   c)*   surface dyslexia.
   d)   deep dyslexia.

22. From the information presented, you would predict that Jane has damage in which area(s) of the brain?

   a)   left frontal and parietal areas
   b)   diffusely throughout the right hemisphere
   c)*   left temporal area
   d)   either the left or the right occipital areas

23. Studies of patients with deep dyslexia and of split-brain patients suggest that lexical access

   a)   is performed in several different areas, all of which are in the left hemisphere.
   b)   is a right-hemisphere process, in contrast to syntactic processing, which is a left-hemisphere process.
   c)   is only impaired by temporal lobe damage.
   d)*   none of the above

24. Split-brain patients are people who had their ___ cut in an attempt to _____.

   a)   frontal lobes; lessen inhibitory effects
   b)   corpus callosum; treat dyslexia
   c)*   corpus callosum; treat epilepsy
   d)   none of the above

25. A word presented in the left visual field

   a)*   goes first to the right hemisphere.
   b)   goes first to the left hemisphere.
   c)   arrives simultaneously at both hemispheres.
   d)   is first processed at the optic chiasm.

Copyright © Houghton Mifflin Company. All rights reserved.

26. Which of the following sentences is most likely to be difficult for a patient with Broca's aphasia to understand fully?

    a)   The chef carved the turkey.
    b)*   The girl called the boy.
    c)   The crane slid down the side of the hill.
    d)   None of the above because Broca's aphasia is a production deficit.

27. According to the trace deletion hypothesis,

    a)   the symptoms of Broca's aphasia are the result of a complete loss of syntactic processing ability.
    b)   Broca's aphasia results from the loss of the connection between the comprehension and production centers for language.
    c)   agrammatism is caused by a loss of the working memory capacity needed to maintain the syntactic memory trace.
    d)*   agrammatism results from loss of information about the movements of elements from their position in the d-structure.

28. If we monitor activity in the brain as we present people with sentences of increasing syntactic complexity, we find an increase of activation

    a)   throughout the whole cortex.
    b)   throughout the left hemisphere.
    c)*   in Broca's area.
    d)   in Wernicke's area.

29. A major difference between capacity theories of agrammatism and the trace deletion hypothesis is that only the trace deletion hypothesis argues that damage to Broca's area results in

    a)   comprehension as well as production deficits.
    b)   damage to a working memory buffer that is specifically dedicated to syntactic processing.
    c)*   loss of syntactic competence.
    d)   all of the above

30. Compared to spoken languages, the syntax of sign languages depends more on

    a)*   spatial location of the symbols.
    b)   the ordering of sentence elements.
    c)   the right hemisphere of the brain.
    d)   all of the above

Chapter 12   115

31. If someone whose native language is American Sign Language suffers from agrammatic aphasia, you would expect to find a lesion in the

    a)   right frontal area.
    b)*   left frontal area.
    c)   right temporal area.
    d)   left temporal area.

32. Which of the following statements regarding the role of the right hemisphere in language is true?

    a)   The right hemisphere plays a role in the integration of discourse but not in the interpretation of individual words.
    b)*   The right hemisphere plays a role in maintaining alternate interpretations of language stimuli.
    c)   The right hemisphere does not perform semantic analysis, but it receives the results of semantic analysis performed by the left hemisphere.
    d)   all of the above.

33. The "right hemisphere syndrome" includes

    a)*   difficulties with understanding metaphoric statements.
    b)   understanding the gist of a passage, but missing the details.
    c)   exaggerated intonation in speech.
    d)   all of the above.

Integrative Essay Questions

1. Discuss the distinction between the terms "related" and "exclusively related" as applied to the study of brain-language relationships. How are these terms related to the idea of modularity? Why are both activation studies and lesion studies needed to determine whether some function is related to a particular brain area?

2. Describe how MRI, fMRI, PET, and evoked potentials are used to study brain-language relationships. What are the strengths and weaknesses of each technique?

3. Draw a sketch of the left hemisphere and label the areas comprising the classic language circuit. How have our ideas about the functions of each of these areas changed over the past 100 years?

4. For which language function(s) is the evidence strongest for localization in a rather restricted area? Describe a function that is not strictly localized. Describe evidence that supports your answer.

Copyright © Houghton Mifflin Company. All rights reserved.

References

Baddley, A. D., & Hitch, G. (1974). Working memory. In G.H. Bower (Ed.), *The psychology of learning and motivation*, Vol. 8 (pp. 47-89). New York: Academic Press.

Clark, H. H. (1996). *Using language.* Cambridge: Cambridge University Press.

Clark, H. H. (1997). Dogmas of understanding. *Discourse Processes, 23,* 567-598.

Dekle, D., Fowler, C. A. & Funnell, M. (1992). Audio-visual integration in perception of real words. *Perception and Psychophysics, 51,* 355-362.

Dupré, J. (Ed.) (1987). *The latest on the best: Essays on evolution and optimality.* Cambridge, MA: MIT Press.

Fodor, J. A., Bever, T. G., & Garrett, M. F. (1974). *The psychology of language: An introduction to psycholinguistics and generative grammar.* New York: McGraw-Hill.

Fowler, C. A., Treiman, R. & Gross, J. (1993). The structure of English syllables and polysyllables. *Journal of Memory and Language, 32,* 115-140.

Gleason, J. Berko (1997). *The development of language. (4th ed.).* Boston: Allyn and Bacon.

Holtgraves, T. (1997). Styles of language use: Individual and cultural variability in conversational indirectness. *Journal of Personality and Social Psychology, 73,* 624-632.

Kim, M. & Bresnahan, M. (1996). Cognitive basis of gender communication: A cross-cultural investigation of perceived constraints in requesting. *Communication Quarterly, 44,* 53-59.

Lenhoff, H. M., Wang, P. P., Greenberg, F., & Bellugi, U. (1997). Williams syndrome and the brain. *Scientific American, 277(6),* 68-73.

Neely, J. H. (1977). Semantic priming and retrieval from lexical memory: Roles of inhibitionless spreading activation and limited-capacity attention. *Journal of Experimental Psychology: General, 106,* 226-254.

Onifer, W., & Swinney, D. A. (1981). Accessing lexical ambiguities during sentence coprehension: Effects of frequency of meaning and contextual bias. *Memory & Cognition, 9,* 225-236.

Pinker, S. (1997). *How the mind works.* New York: Norton.

Reder, L. M., & Kusbit, G. W. (1991). Locus of the Moses illusion: Imperfect encoding, retrieval, or match? *Journal of Memory and Language, 30,* 385-406.

Copyright © Houghton Mifflin Company. All rights reserved.

van Dijk, T. A. (1984). *Prejudice in discourse.* Amsterdam: Benjamins.

van Dijk, T. A. (1987). *Communicating racism.* Newbury Park, CA: Sage.

van Dijk, T. A. (1997). *Elite discourse and racism..* Newbury Park, CA: Sage.